PAPIER MÂCHÉ
·STYLE·

ALEX MacCORMICK

Photographs by
MICHAEL HARVEY

PAPIER MÂCHÉ STYLE

■ *100 step-by-step designs*

**Krause Publications
Iola, Wisconsin**

For my brother and sister,
Neil MacCormick and Fionna Cardale,
with love.

Published by Krause Publications, Iola, Wisconsin

ISBN 0-8019-8755-5

Edited by Veronica Sperling
Designed by Yvonne Dedman
Technical advice by Amanda Godden
Typeset by Florencetype Ltd, Stoodleigh, Devon
Printed & bound in Slovenia by Printing House DELO-Tiskarna
by arrangement with Korotan Ljubljana

ACKNOWLEDGEMENTS

The author and publishers would like to thank the following
for their generous help:

All the gifted artists listed on page 127 who made and
loaned their work to be photographed for this book; photog-
rapher Michael Harvey and assistant Jeremy Murch for fun
and expertise in the studio; Amanda Godden, our technical
adviser, who also made most of the papier mâché pieces in
the Basic Techniques section; Melanie Williams for making
the chickenwire pigs for the section on Basic Techniques;
Sybilla Lewyska and Bridget Garrett for painting backgrounds
and bases; Valerie Wade Antiques, 108 Fulham Road, London
SW3 6HS, for the illustration on p. 6 and for the loan of the
box on p. 8; Sarah Beales of Nomad Art, 791 Fulham Road,
London SW6, Davina Instone of Crocodile Leap, 15 Bellevue
Road, London SW17 7EG, and Sally Bryant of 7 + 7 Interiors,
91 Northcote Road, London SW11 6PL, for the loan of papier
mâché pieces by various makers.

Finally, the author would like to thank editors David
Roberts and Alison Bell, and copy-editor Veronica Sperling.

**Half-title page: Bowls
(Carol Hill)**

**Title page: Vases and
bowls (Maureen Hamilton-
Hill)**

**Contents page: Handmade
sheet (Carol Hill)**

·CONTENTS·

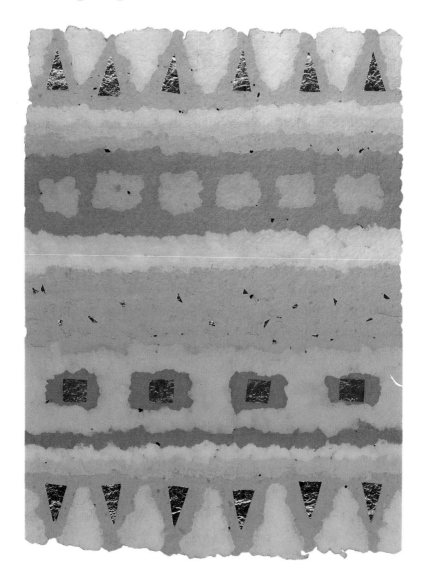

·INTRODUCTION·

Papier mâché invites imaginative experiment – there are no unbreakable rules, no restrictions, no prescribed traditions. It may look like metal, wood or porcelain, yet, when you pick up even a large paper object, it is always surprisingly light. Papier mâché has a certain magical allure few can resist: rather like an alchemist turning base metal into gold, you can transform mundane ingredients into beautiful and useful objects.

Over the last few years there has been a tremendous revival of interest in this artistic craft, and its creative possibilities are once more being recognized. The appeal of papier mâché rests on three main factors. Firstly, it is great fun because it is easy to make, and is both soothing and inspiring to work with. Secondly, this is a very versatile medium, which can be used to shape anything from a dinosaur or a giant sculpture, through furnishings such as chairs, clocks, cupboards, mirror frames and lamps to delicate jewelry, dolls, vases, masks and chess pieces. Thirdly, the basic materials required are inexpensive and readily available, often in your own home – newspapers, string and surplus cardboard packaging, for instance.

The opportunity to recycle materials is particularly appealing to those who care about conservation and do not have money to throw away. This was also the case in centuries past.

Although it is widely believed that the name 'papier mâché' comes from the French words *papier* (paper) and *mâcher* (to chew), recent research indicates that the term most likely derives from the English verb 'to mash' or mix with water and the pronunciation of the words was simply garbled over the years. No matter what the correct derivation, people have taken the trouble to conserve and recycle paper ever since it was first invented in China, it is said, early in the second century AD.

The skills developed by the Chinese in moulding such articles as warriors' helmets and pots from papier mâché hardened with lacquer gradually spread along the routes of traders and warring armies eastward to Japan and Korea, and westward in the eighth century via Samarkand to Damascus in what is now Syria.

Once the Arabs learned how to recycle waste material, including valuable paper, the techniques were slowly disseminated as far afield as Morocco in North Africa.

By the eleventh century such knowledge extended into Europe through France and Spain. However, it appears that the Italians learned the craft by a more direct route – from Venetian merchants who traded in the Far East – and, in turn, the Italians taught craftsmen in Persia and India how to decorate papier mâché in the Florentine style with flowers and foliage. Such designs are still commonly seen today on objects made in Kashmir and elsewhere in the sub-continent.

In the East, where lacquering and decorating papier mâché became a highly prized art form, pieces were for centuries only made to order for aristocratic patrons and so were not available for export. It was not until the sixteenth century, therefore, that the first examples of such work were brought to Europe by Portuguese merchants and, later, by Dutchmen, from whom English travellers purchased cabinets and screens to take home. In 1600 the English East India Company set up trade links with Japan, China and India, and within fifteen years its first ship returned laden with Japanese 'scritoires [desks], trunkes, beoubes [screens], cups and dishes of all sorts and of a most excellent varnish'.

It was this 'most excellent varnish', highly polished and hard wearing, as well as the beautifully painted decoration beneath, which excited the interest of European collectors and eventually makers alike. The resin of trees indigenous to the Far East which formed the lacquer was difficult to duplicate in the West and so it was not until late in the seventeenth century that European makers met with much success in what became known as 'japanning'. In the meantime, the rarity and cost of imported oriental black lacquer ware – generally termed 'Japan ware' no matter whether it came from China, Japan or India – had created a fashionable market in which demand far exceeded supply.

To meet this need workshops and, later, factories were set up in various countries including France, Britain, Germany and Russia. Many major innovations originated in France, where in the mid-eighteenth century papier mâché was used to imitate plaster and stucco decorations on ceilings and walls, and to form objets d'art and furniture. French influence swiftly crossed the borders to other countries, in particular Germany,

◀ **A selection of antique papier mâché (Valerie Wade)**

which in the 1800s became famous for its sophisticated papier mâché dolls' heads, and to England, where the greatest scale of production was achieved.

Between 1770 and 1870 the craft was at its peak in terms of artistry, production and sales. Birmingham and Wolverhampton in the British Midlands became the prime centres. In 1788 one Charles Ducrest was granted a patent for 'making paper for the building of houses, bridges, ships, boats and all sorts of wheel carriages, sedan chairs, tables and book cases, either entirely of paper, or wood and iron covered in paper'. The range of products made from papier mâché increased considerably and by 1850 it was said that 'few houses can now be found in which some useful and elegant trifle may not be seen made of this exquisite material'.

From Britain and other European countries both goods and expertise were transmitted to the USA, where in 1850 the Litchfield Manufacturing Company set up the first factory for lacquered papier mâché in Litchfield, Connecticut. There followed the foundation of several other factories, in Connecticut and in Boston, Mass. In the late 1890s an Act of Congress even permitted the maceration of withdrawn banknotes to create commercial pulp – which was then moulded into replicas of national monuments and busts of eminent Americans. Nowadays these mottled grey ornaments are collectors' items.

By 1920 public tastes had changed and the last manufacturer of papier mâché in England had ceased trading. Until recently this remarkable craft was largely forgotten in the West, except in those few schools where young children were encouraged to struggle with gluey fingers over lumpen dishes and animals. Now, nearly 1800 years after paper was first invented, we are able to participate in the exciting renaissance of papier mâché.

In the following twenty-nine pages practical advice is offered on the basic materials, equipment and techniques used by craftspeople today. Do, please, spare the time to read these sections before launching into your first project if you wish to achieve the most satisfactory results. On the subsequent eighty-nine pages you will find invaluable guidance and stunning illustrations of some of the myriad ways in which you, like the makers whose work is shown in this book, can create your own Papier Mâché Style.

◄ **Kashmiri box, 1869
(Valerie Wade)**

BASIC EQUIPMENT ·AND MATERIALS·

You will find that most of the materials and equipment required for creating papier mâché objects are readily available in your own home or from local craft/art supplies shops. This list illustrates some of the basic requirements; a few more specialized ingredients are listed, where appropriate, at the start of a project.

■ WORK SURFACE

You need a large flat area where work can be left undisturbed. Cover the surface in plastic sheeting or with opened out supermarket plastic carrier bags to protect the work top and prevent objects from sticking to it.

■ PAPER

Newspapers – broadsheets are better quality paper than tabloids; pink plus white ones are useful for distinguishing layers; tear into pieces, never cut with scissors.
Wall-lining paper – cheap and effective torn into pieces, especially as a final layer for painting on.
Blotting paper, brown wrapping paper, cartridge paper, sugar paper – coloured or plain, strong and particularly effective over large areas.
Gummed paper tape – quick and strong over small areas (see the sconce on page 106).
Tissue paper, paper napkins, crêpe paper – translucent and ideal for creasing into textured surfaces.
Handmade paper – your own (see page 34) or shop bought comes in a variety of weights and textures, has infinite uses and gives a distinguished finish to objects. *See also* Other Decorative Ingredients, page 12.

■ ADHESIVES

Non-toxic paste powder – safe for children.
Wallpaper paste – takes a while to dry, but easy to use when layering paper (see page 13); any type of gesso, traditional or acrylic, may be used on top of it (see Primers page 12).
Flour and water paste – inexpensive for layering paper, but may go lumpy and later grow mould.
PVA (polyvinyl acetate) wood glue/white glue – stronger for fastening paper to wood or metal and for joining cardboard pieces; in diluted form as a sealant to prevent cardboard, etc, from warping; and acrylic gesso is best used on top of it.

Rabbit-skin size – made from granules mixed with water, may be used instead of PVA/white glue if you want to paint an object with traditional gesso (see page 36).
Epoxy resin – can be used as a substitute for varnish or for very strong joins, but not for use by children and not easy for layering paper.
Vegetable glue – most suitable for adding material to finished objects, e.g. lining a box with fabric.

■ TAPES

Masking tape – fixes plastic wrap/saran wrap round a mould and secures glued joins until they are dry, when it is best replaced by gummed paper tape, though some makers do not bother.
Gummed paper tape – strengthens glued joins and is occasionally used instead of layers of pasted paper pieces (see page 106).
Gummed plastic parcel tape – useful for securing joins of large wooden moulds.

■ PASTE BOWL

Virtually any kind of mixing bowl – plastic, glass or porcelain – is suitable for mixing wallpaper paste or holding diluted PVA/white glue, etc. In a container with an airtight lid or sealed with plastic wrap/saran wrap, paste will last for several days.

■ MOULDS AND FRAMEWORKS

Many household objects (see following page) make suitable moulds for layering paper upon (see page 13), but bear in mind that, if the object narrows at any point, you may have to cut the papier mâché in half with a scalpel to remove it:
Balloons – of any shape or size are good for layering paper upon (see page 17).
Smooth-sided cardboard with corrugated interior, corrugated cardboard, flexible cardboard, rigid or flexible sheets of card – useful as basis for boxes, puppet theatre, mirror or picture frames, brooches, bracelets, etc; re-use old packaging whenever possible.
Modelling clay/plastic (plasticine) – used for shaping into objects to cast in a plaster mould (see page 27) or for creating details with/without layered paper on top.

Bowl of wallpaper paste

Pencil and felt pen

Artists' brushes

Household paint brush

White emulsion paint (primer)

Petroleum jelly (releasing agent)

Masking tape

Balloons (for moulds)

Metal ruler/cutting edge

Cardboard, pink and white newspapers, cartridge or sugar paper

Scalpel

Modelling plastic

Scissors

Craft knife with retractable blade

Wrapping paper, tissue paper, foil and photocopy (decoration)

Gouache paints (decoration)

Polyurethane varnish (sealer)

PVA/white glue

Plastic wrap/saran wrap (releasing agent)

Chickenwire – for creating an armature with pulp or layered paper on top (see page 30) and with a wooden substructure for larger pieces, e.g. lamp on page 90.

Wood – provides a strong framework for chickenwire armatures, for shelves, cupboards, etc, and for creating large frames to hold plaster/gypsum for moulds.

Plaster of Paris/gypsum – for creating moulds (see page 27).

■ RELEASING AGENTS

These prevent pulp or pasted paper from adhering to a mould:

Plastic wrap/saran wrap – comes in a roll, is secured in place with masking tape, and is used on simple shapes such as bowls, trays, woks, etc.

Petroleum jelly – most useful on intricate moulds or when you do not mind being left with a greasy surface to the papier mâché. Always remove any excess, otherwise it will cause difficulty later when you come to paint and decorate.

Soft soap or washing-up liquid – alternative to petroleum jelly.

■ FILLERS

Used to add bulk to paper pulp (see page 25):

Ground chalk/whiting – available from chemists and craft shops, it is the most commonly used filler.

Fine sawdust – may be used half and half with ground chalk/whiting, or as a cheap substitute for it.

■ CUTTERS

All of the following will be useful at one time or another:

Scissors, scalpel and a craft knife with a retractable blade – useful for a variety of purposes; special paper scissors are advisable.

Wire-cutters/tin-snips – for cutting wire and chickenwire.

Pair of pliers – for shaping chickenwire and wire.

Saws – a handsaw for lengths or planks of wood, and a jigsaw for cutting out intricate shapes.

Liquidizer/blender – for making pulp (see page 25).

■ MARKERS

A soft pencil and/or a fine felt-tip pen are needed for marking cutting lines and for outlining decorative designs on white emulsion or other sealant primers before painting.

◀ **Some basic equipment**

■ METAL RULER

For measuring and as a safe cutting edge.

■ SANDPAPER/GLASSPAPER

For smoothing out imperfections and improving adhesion in the course of applying layers of primer or before final paint decoration.

■ PRIMERS

These are brushed on top of a paper object to provide a smooth white surface on which to paint, but a primer is not necessary if you intend to use decorative paper as your top layer:

Matt water-based household white emulsion paint – the most commonly used and economical primer.

Traditional gesso – contains rabbit-skin size (see recipe on page 36) and provides a hard, chalky surface for painting. It is best used on paper objects made with wallpaper paste.

Acrylic gesso – available from shops in powder or liquid form, is best used when a paper object is made with lots of PVA/white glue.

■ PAINTS

Almost any kind of paint, crayon or pastel may be used for decorating, including:

Water-bound paints – such as watercolours, emulsions, poster paints, powder paints, gouaches, acrylics and watercolour pastels, crayons or sticks.

Oil-bound media – such as oil crayons and pastels, oil glazes, metallic and pearlized paints, but very rarely oil paint *per se*.

Transfer or water-gilded metal leaf or foil.

Bole – powdered clay in various colours.

■ INK

Waterproof ink – in a felt-tip pen or Indian ink applied with a fine brush is used for outlines, details, etc.

■ OTHER DECORATIVE INGREDIENTS

Modelling plastic/plasticine, modelling clay and string – for creating raised decorative features or details.

Photocopies – black-and-white ones hand coloured present endless possibilities, especially for those who are not particularly dextrous with an artist's brush.

Wrapping paper – can be used in large pieces to cover smooth areas; marbled paper achieves a *trompe l'oeil* effect; torn to create a patchwork effect or roses, leaves, etc used as découpage.

Foil paper – from sweet wrappers or cigarette packets can be highly decorative.

Coloured cartridge paper or sugar paper – torn up, the edges soak up extra varnish or oil glaze to create a marbled effect.

Dried/pressed plant material – flowers, leaves, stalks, etc can be incorporated in handmade paper or glued on to a painted surface.

Fabric – may be incorporated as small pieces of e.g. silk in handmade paper, used to line boxes, etc, or larger pieces can comprise a complete decorative layer, smooth or wrinkled.

■ SEALERS

It is wise to give a protective coat to papier mâché work:

Polyurethane clear wood varnish – comes in matt, semi-gloss or gloss finishes, and is waterproof and hard wearing.

Yacht varnish – comes in gloss only, is durable and cheap, but yellows quite quickly especially over pale colours.

Acrylic varnish – the water-based version is quick drying, tough and very clear.

Paper lacquer or varnish – matt, available from craft shops, and does not discolour pale or delicate paper.

Linseed oil – brush on three or four coats and bake the object in an oven at a temperature not exceeding 130°C (250°F) until dry to give a hard, waterproof surface.

Bees' wax – rub it on with your fingertips for a gentle gleam.

Car spray lacquer – a quick way to apply a durable, glossy sealant.

Fire retardant – in a spray or liquid form, vital on candlesticks, wall sconces, etc; it is sometimes incorporated in certain makes of varnish, but is liable to discolour, so try it out first on something which does not matter.

Water repellant – invisible coating as an additional insurance on top of paper varnish.

■ BRUSHES

Household paint brushes – several of various size will be needed for applying primer, gesso, varnish, etc.

Artists' watercolour brushes – of hair or nylon, you will need three for decorating: one large, one medium and one fine.

·BASIC TECHNIQUES·

■ LAYERING PAPER ON AN EXISTING MOULD

Laminating or layering paper is the first technique most people learn because it is simple, versatile and relatively strong.

You are going to build one layer upon another and a handy method of keeping track of how many layers you have done is to use one layer of pink broadsheet newspaper followed by a layer of ordinary white broadsheet newspaper and so on, or one layer of newspaper followed by a layer of wall-lining paper. This 'trick' is especially useful if you are likely to be interrupted.

Most papier mâché makers prefer to tear the paper rather than cut it because you end up with a smoother finish and the paper knits together more strongly. The strips or squares should be roughly uniform in size, depending on the size of object you are making.

EQUIPMENT AND MATERIALS

Plastic sheeting or plastic bags	Bowl of wallpaper paste
	Craft knife
Mould, e.g. bowl or dish	PVA/white glue or gesso (optional)
Plastic wrap/saran wrap or petroleum jelly	Emulsion paint (primer sealant)
Masking tape	
Newspaper and/or wall-lining paper	Paint brushes, various
	Materials for decorating
Damp cloth (for wiping)	Sealer, e.g. varnish

METHOD Cover your work surface preferably with plastic sheeting, or at least with newspapers (things stick more easily to the latter than the former).

If you are going to use wallpaper paste, now is the moment to mix an appropriate quantity in a bowl, following the maker's instructions. Allow a few minutes for it to thicken to the consistency of thick cream.

So that you can later extract the finished object from the mould, you must cover the mould including its edges and rim with a releasing agent such as plastic wrap/saran wrap or petroleum jelly (remember to remove any excess). The plastic/saran wrap must be spread as smoothly and closely as possible to the mould, and fixed with masking tape. (If you are going to make the mould an integral part of the finished object, say for jewelry or a piece of furniture, omit the releasing agent.)

Tear your paper into strips of appropriate length (experience will teach you what this is), dip each piece into the paste and gently remove any excess by sliding the paper between your fingers. Apply the pieces at varying angles with each piece slightly overlapping the next until the whole of the inside of the mould is covered. Do not put the pieces in regular rows as this gives rise to lines of weakness round or across the object. Smooth out any air bubbles as they can spoil the look of a finished piece. If the paper starts sliding around, it is probably because you are using too much paste. Do not worry if the paper goes above or over the rim as this can be trimmed off later, if necessary.

Apply the second layer in the opposite direction to the first, making sure that the first layer is completely covered. (continued on page 16)

▲ Affixing plastic/saran wrap with tape

▲ Applying the second layer of paper

◄ A selection of moulds
on which to layer paper

At this point some people prefer to let the work dry between the application of each subsequent layer, but there is no vital necessity to do so; it simply means the object will dry more quickly.

Add the next and subsequent layers in alternate directions. If the object you are making is going to have a lid, check that the lid will still fit before adding further layers.

After six layers done in one sitting, it is advisable to let the object dry over a couple of days before proceeding.

The number of layers you choose to apply depends not only on how thick you want the finished object to be and the thickness of the paper being used but also on whether you intend strengthening it with a priming coat of gesso (see page 36) and/or a hard varnish sealant (see page 12). Experimentation is part of the fun!

Papier mâché is least likely to buckle when left to dry naturally on a cake rack in a warm room or in an airing cupboard for two or three days; some makers, however, 'bake' their work in a conventional oven or a microwave (no metallic moulds) in a low to medium setting until dry. Again timing is a matter of experience.

When you have as many layers as you require and the object has dried out, remove it from the mould by twisting it gently. If it gets stuck, try to ease round the edge with a palette knife; if that does not work, you may have to cut the paper with a craft knife or scalpel and then repair the damage with PVA/white glue and more papier mâché. If you wish to add a rim, spout, handle, base, etc, this is the stage at which to do so (see pages 18–25).

If you want to give the object a hard surface and prevent warping or paint from spreading, you can seal it with a thin coat of PVA/white glue or a layer of acrylic or traditional gesso (see page 36).

When the vessel is dry, coat it with emulsion paint. When this primer is dry, the object is ready to decorate.

When the decorated object is completely dry, apply a coat of sealer such as matt or gloss varnish (see page 12).

◀ **Decorating with pieces of wrapping paper**

■ LAYERING PAPER OVER A BALLOON

Balloons make versatile moulds because they come in many shapes and sizes. Long ones can, for instance, be used for creating cylindrical vases or cut into sections for bracelets, while with round ones you can make bowls, jugs or vases large and small. There is a chance that the balloon may burst once it is covered in papier mâché so take protective measures!

EQUIPMENT AND MATERIALS

Plastic sheeting or plastic bags	Newspaper and/or wall-lining paper
Bowl of wallpaper paste	Cup/small bowl (as stand for drying)
Balloon	Scissors or craft knife

METHOD Cover your work surface with plastic so that the sticky balloon will not adhere to it or, if you prefer to work with the balloon on your lap, then cover that with an old plastic carrier bag.

Mix the wallpaper paste in a bowl following the maker's instructions.

Blow up the balloon and tie a knot in the neck.

Rip the paper into strips or squares of appropriate size. Dip each piece in the paste, remove the excess with your fingers and smooth it on to the balloon, over-lapping each piece slightly.

If you are making a bowl, start from the bottom of the balloon and work upwards, stopping when you have reached the desired height.

If you are making a vase or a jug, you can start papering from the top downwards.

Once the first layer is completed, you can either set this aside to dry before continuing or you can proceed to add further layers. But, if the paper layers start to slip around out of position, stop. Remove any excess paste and paper until the layers are stable, and then let it all dry out thoroughly before resuming work.

Altogether you will need to cover the desired area with about eight layers of paper to create a substantial object.

If you want to make a flat-bottomed bowl, bravely puncture the balloon when the paper is almost dry but still damp, and slap the bottom of the bowl on a flat surface. Alternative methods are given on page 21.

For anything else, however, wait until the papier mâché is thoroughly dry before removing the balloon by unting the knot or bursting it with a pin. Trim the rim with scissors, if appropriate.

If you are making a bowl, see pages 21 and 18 for instructions on how to create a base and appropriate rim.

▲ Applying the third layer on a balloon

▲ Trimming a rim with scissors

If you are making a vase, for the top opening either cut a hole in the paper with scissors or gently rip the paper open with your fingers and remove the balloon. Then follow the directions on pages 21 and 20 for making a base and neck.

Once any additional features have been added (base, rim, etc), the dried papier mâché is ready for sealing, if you so wish, with PVA/white glue or with layers of gesso (see page 36), an optional primer coat of white emulsion paint, decorating and finally sealing with varnish (see page 12).

■ **RIMS**

Simple Rims Using a ruler with its end on a flat surface beside the object to be trimmed, mark on the vessel's flat surface at a number of points round it the exact same height. Join these points with a continuous free-hand line, making the edging line as even as possible. Then trim the edge with scissors or a craft knife.

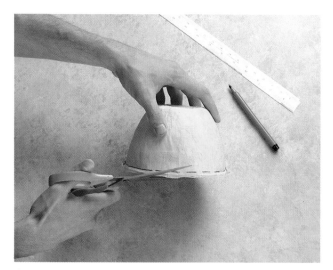

▲ **Trimming a simple rim**

Narrow Lip To neaten a bowl or similar with a lipped edge remove the object from the mould, trim the outer edge of the lip with scissors or a craft knife and then neaten the cut edge by pasting over it small strips of paper.

When the paper is dry, work lightly on the surface with sandpaper to get it smooth, first with medium grade sandpaper/glasspaper and then fine grade.

▲ **How to neaten a narrow lip or edge**

Rounded Lip There are several alternative ways of making a rounded lip – using plastic tubing/pipe, haberdashery cord or coarse string (the texture of which adds a decorative feature), or thin paper rolls. Whatever you decide to use, make sure that the thickness will suit the proportions of the existing paper object and that it is pliable enough to fit the curve of the rim.

The method described below can also be used on a vessel without a lip (i.e. clean cut) or to decorate other areas of any object.

Tuck the tubing, cord, string or two paper rolls at a time under the trimmed lip of the bowl or similar object and hold it/them in position with one hand while sticking the end of a longish pasted paper strip or piece of masking tape on to the outside of the object just below the tubing/cord, etc, over the tubing/cord, etc, and on to the inside.

▲ **Pasting paper over tubing for a rounded lip**

▲ **Neatening the outside of a rounded lip**

BASIC TECHNIQUES

18

Once the tubing/cord/string/paper rolls are firmly held in place, apply two layers of narrow pasted paper strips over the rim until it looks neat. Use thin paper if you want the texture of the cord or string to show through.

Broad, Flat Rim To add a broad, flat rim to a bowl, for instance, or to create a hat, turn the vessel upside down on to a sheet of cardboard, and carefully draw round the rim with a pencil. Then sketch on the cardboard the exact size of the outer edge of the new rim you wish to add, using a pair of compasses, if necessary, for precision. Before cutting, check that the proportion and size of the new rim will suit the existing object.

Cut the rim of the cardboard with scissors or a craft knife and place it on top of the vessel's rim. When it is in the right position, secure it in place with tape or PVA/white glue.

Some makers then fill the junction of the rim and bowl shape with paper pulp inside and out, but a simpler, quicker and equally strong option is to use modelling plastic (plasticine).

Place the bowl with its cardboard rim face down on the work surface. Mould strips of modelling plastic roughly into a triangular shape and press them delicately into the junction. Even out the surface and edges of the plastic with your fingers so that the joins are seamless. Then cover the plastic and the flat rim inside and out with at least three layers of pasted paper pieces, paying particular attention to achieving a smooth outer rim. As soon as the paper layers are dry the object can be emulsioned, decorated and varnished; the oiliness of the plastic does not affect the process.

As a much weaker alternative you can attach the cardboard rim to the vessel with tape and then paste on several layers of thin, overlapping strips of paper running from inside the vessel, over the rim and on to the vessel beneath the rim. Then, to conceal the ends of the strips which are holding the rim in place, paste a band of small strips parallel to the rim inside and out.

■ NECKS

You may wish to add a neck or funnel to a vase, for instance, rather than leave a plain opening.

Turn the vessel upside down on to a sheet of thin cardboard or thickish card and mark round the vessel's opening with a pencil. Then draw on the cardboard or card the depth and shape of the neck or funnel you want. With scissors or a craft knife cut out the shape and make a cut from outer rim to inner rim, fold the cardboard into a circle and place it just inside the opening of the vessel.

Check that the size and shape are what you desire before taping the new neck together and to the vessel.

Add at least three layers of papier mâché in long, thin, overlapping strips over the cardboard on the joint with the vessel both inside and out. If necessary, cover the ends of these strips by pasting a band of small strips parallel to the neck on the outside of the vase.

▲ **Attaching a funnel neck**

◀ **Pasting over the neck**

◼ BASES

Flat Bases There are four simple alternative methods of creating flat bases for rounded objects such as bowls and vases which have been moulded on balloons, etc.

1. If you are feeling brave, you can remove the vessel from its mould or balloon while it is still slightly damp and slap its bottom firmly on to a flat surface. Leave it to dry on a cake rack or similar. This is obviously a rather hit-and-miss method and requires confidence.

2. Cut out a couple of circles of suitable size from cardboard, and in the base of the vessel cut a slightly smaller hole. Fix the cardboard circles one on top of the other to the base of the vessel with tape and then cover them with several layers of pasted strips of paper. (There is no need to cover them and paint them before affixing them as the maker chose to do in the illustration.) Hide the rough ends of these strips by pasting over them a band of small strips running parallel to the new base.

3. Cut a strip of card or flexible cardboard to the required length, bend it into a circle (like a dog collar) fixed with masking tape, then tape this circlet to the base of the vessel. Finally cover it with layers of pasted paper strips as for method 2.

4. Cut the bottom off the paper vessel and then from cardboard or thick card cut a circle to fill the hole. Fix this in place with masking tape. Tear strips of paper long enough to reach from one side of the cardboard circle to the other and on to the vessel. Paste a layer in one direction over the opening, overlapping each piece. Apply the next layer at right angles to the first, and so on for each subsequent layer. You will need at least three layers. Disguise the ends of these strips by pasting over them a band of small strips running parallel to the base.

▲ Method 2

▲ Method 3

▲ Method 4

BASIC TECHNIQUES

21

▼ Attaching a splayed base

Footed Base There are several ways of making a footed base for vessels such as a bowl or a vase, but here is the most basic.

Choose a small bowl to use as a mould and double check that its size will suit the vessel of which this will form the base. Following the method described on page 00, build up eight layers of pasted paper, firming them in place round the rim and allowing them to protrude beyond the edge by about 2.5cm(1in).

The papier mâché must be completely dry before it is removed from the mould. Trim the edge of the rim with scissors or a craft knife and then neaten the cut edge by pasting over it small strips of paper to create a smooth surface.

To create a rounded lip for the foot, follow the instructions on page 18.

Turn the small bowl upside down and glue its base firmly to the base of the larger vessel. To disguise the join you can then, if you wish, apply plastic tubing, cord, string or paper rolls, using the same techniques as for a rounded lip (see page 18) and pushing the material well into the join. As before, cover the ridge created with several layers of small paper strips.

If you decide not to disguise the join, simply cover the junction with several layers of pasted paper strips or pieces, pushing the paper carefully into the waist as much or as little as you wish.

Splayed Base The way in which you build a splayed base is very similar to the method used for creating the neck of a vase (see page 20).

Cut a strip of card or cardboard to the depth you require, bend it into a circle which is broader at the bottom than the top (like a cone with its head lopped off) and fix it together with PVA/white glue or tape. Then tape or glue the narrow side of the circlet to the bottom of the existing bowl, vase or whatever.

Apply at least three layers of long pasted paper strips over the join between the bowl and the new base as well as to the new base itself, both inside and out. To neaten the ends of these strips, paste a band of small strips end to end parallel to the base.

■ HANDLES

When considering what shape and size of handle to make, you must first decide whether it is to be a purely decorative feature or whether it will need to be strong enough to lift the finished object full or empty. Then make sketches of suitable handles.

For a decorative handle make a full-size pattern of your chosen shape from cardboard including a tab at top and bottom.

If you want a flat handle, simply cover the cardboard with several layers of pasted paper strips, leaving the tabs uncovered.

If, however, you want a rounded handle, use a piece of rubber tubing of appropriate length and diameter. At both ends of the tubing make two 1cm (½in) slits with a craft knife and splay out the tubing into two 'tabs' at each end.

Using a craft knife, cut two slots in the vessel in the precise positions where the handle tabs are to be inserted. Insert the tabs into the slots and cover the joints inside and out with masking tape and three or more layers of pasted paper pieces. Allow to dry completely before sealing or decorating.

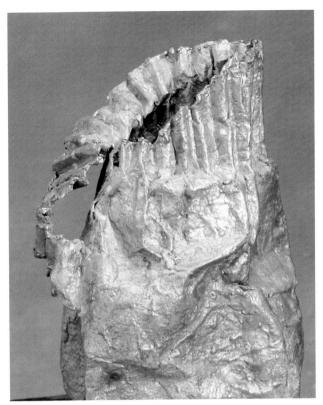

▲ **Detail of pleated handle (Miriam Troth)**

▶ **Securing tabs on the inside with tape**

▼ **Applying pulp to a chickenwire handle**

For a stronger handle roll a piece of chicken wire into a tube of appropriate length and diameter and carefully tuck away any spiky ends along its length. Bend the roll of chicken wire into the desired shape.

Using a craft knife, cut two slots in the vessel in the precise positions where the ends of the handle are to be inserted. Insert the ends into the holes, check that the shape of the handle is what you wish, and carefully splay the ends inside the vessel to hold the handle in place.

Cover the chicken wire with several layers of paper pulp (see page 25), allowing each to dry before adding the next, or bind the chickenwire with overlapping strips of pasted paper in four or more layers. Remember to cover with pulp or pasted strips the exposed wire ends inside the vessel as well to make the joint secure. Allow to dry thoroughly before decorating.

■ SPOUTS

Cut a piece of cardboard or sturdy card into a triangle with three equal sides. Bend it gently in half. The folded edge of this V-shape will form the spout, so attach the pointed end of the V to the vessel with tape or PVA/white glue. Trim any excess from the point of the spout with a craft knife.

Cover the junction of the spout and the vessel with modelling plastic carefully smoothed into place inside and out to create a strong, neat join. Then cover the whole area with at least three layers of pasted paper pieces. Allow the paper to dry out before coating with emulsion or PVA/white glue and decorating.

▲ **Attaching a spout with tape**

▲ **Modelling plastic covering the junction**

■ HOW TO MAKE PULP

EQUIPMENT AND MATERIALS

Large mixing bowl	Liquidizer/blender
4 sheets A2-size paper (broadsheet newspapers/coloured paper/wall-lining paper, etc)	2 tbs **PVA**/white glue
	I tbs linseed oil
	2 tbs mixed wallpaper paste
Water	I tbs ground chalk/whiting (filler)
Large saucepan	

METHOD Tear the paper into pieces no larger than 2.5cm (1in) square. Put the pieces in a mixing bowl, cover with water and leave to soak overnight.

Drain the soaked paper and boil it in a saucepan with 2 litres (3¼pints) of water for twenty minutes. Leave to cool.

Liquidize/blend the paper until it is the desired texture and strain the pulp by squeezing it gently between your hands, but ensure it is not too dry because this makes it difficult to work with. (At this point turn to page 34 if you wish to make sheets of paper.)

Put the pulp into a mixing bowl and add the PVA/white glue, linseed oil, wallpaper paste and ground chalk/whiting. Stir thoroughly. Left unsealed, this mix will be usable for up to two days, but it will last longer if kept in a sealed container.

White or off-white pulp can be dyed a wide range of colours with the type of cold-water dye recommended for use on cotton or viscose fabrics. Stunning effects can also be created by the judicious addition of sparkling or textured threads pulled from old clothes or scraps of material.

▲ **Pulp bowl (Sue Sanders)**

■ USING PULP WITH AN EXISTING MOULD

Beginners are recommended to start by moulding pulp on the inside of simple shapes like bowls, woks or dishes. As you progress, however, you will discover that a whole host of other shapes can be used for moulding on the *outside* by cutting open the papier mâché to release the mould and repairing the join with pulp.

EQUIPMENT AND MATERIALS

Mould, e.g. bowl/wok/dish	**Palette knife (optional)**
Releasing agent – plastic	**Roll of kitchen paper/**
wrap/saran wrap or	**disposable cellulose**
petroleum jelly	**cleaning cloths**
Bowl of pulp (see recipe	
on page 25)	

METHOD Cover the inside of the mould, including the rim, with plastic wrap/saran wrap or petroleum jelly as smoothly as possible.

Apply the pulp in handfuls to the inside of the mould, pressing it firmly in place with your fingers or a palette knife. Once the inside of the mould is completely covered, press the pulp even more firmly into place using a length of kitchen paper or a cleaning cloth rolled into a smooth ball. This removes excess moisture and compacts the pulp evenly.

To create a smooth rim, if so desired, any excess pulp can be carefully trimmed with a palette knife. Or, like pastry, you can create a frilly edge by pinching the pulp between thumb and forefinger, or pattern the edge by pressing a coarse wooden fork against it.

Leave the pulp object to dry for up to a week or so, depending on its thickness, in a warm place such as an airing cupboard before removing it from the mould. (Experienced makers sometimes remove the pulp object from the mould before or during drying, but this is perhaps a little risky for a novice.)

▲ **Attaching pulp to the mould**

▲ **Pinching pulp creates a frilly rim**

Once out of the mould any dents or cracks can easily be repaired by smoothing on more paper pulp. Let the repair dry before, if you wish to do so, rubbing it down with fine sandpaper/glasspaper.

If you wish to seal the object rather than leave it textured (see Carol Hill's bowls on page 42 and left), paint on a thin coat of PVA/white glue or one or more thin layers of gesso (see page 36). Finally the object is ready for decorating.

◀ **Pinched rim on pulp bowl (Carol Hill)**

■ HOW TO MAKE A PLASTER MOULD

Plaster moulds are basically not difficult to make, though some skill may be required if you intend to sculpt modelling clay into an object to replicate rather than simply copy the existing object. However, once made, a mould can save time and trouble, particularly if you wish to produce an object in quantity, such as earrings, small picture frames, masks, etc.

If you wish to create an object without a flat back, one shaped on both sides, make a plaster mould of half of it, use that to cast it twice in pulp and then glue the two halves together with PVA/white glue.

EQUIPMENT AND MATERIALS

Decorator's paint tray/ gardener's plastic seed tray or similar	Materials and equipment for making paper pulp (see page 25)
Object to cast mould from, e.g. a mask	Primer – white emulsion paint or gesso
Petroleum jelly	Paints, etc, for decorating
Mixing bowl	Sealant – varnish or similar
Plaster of Paris/gypsum	
Water	

METHOD Cover evenly the inside of the plastic tray and the outside of the object to be copied (in this instance a mask) with a coating of petroleum jelly. Make sure it goes into any crevices, and remove any excess.

In a mixing bowl make a thick, creamy mix of the powdered plaster/gypsum with water in approximately the following proportions: 1.25kg (2¾lb) powder to 1litre (1¾pints) water. (Alternatively gently pour the powder into the water until a peak appears above the surface, then leave for one minute to allow the dispersal of any trapped air.) Stir thoroughly, but do not whip it or air bubbles will be introduced. Gently pour the mixture into the plastic tray. Immediately rinse the mixing bowl and stirring implement before the plaster/gypsum hardens.

On the inside of the mask cover any openings with waterproof tape. As the plaster loses its sheen, begins to thicken and you can feel it giving off warmth (i.e. it is 'going off' as the professionals say), gently press the face of the mask into the mixture. Do not let the plaster flow over into the inside. When the plaster/gypsum is absolutely cold and hard, it is set. Remove the mask or object being copied.

Leave the mould for a day to ensure it is dry right through before giving the inner surface one or more protective coats of water-based varnish.

Always cover the inside of the mould with petroleum jelly before filling it with either pulp or layers of pasted paper pieces. Remember, too, that paper objects made in such moulds will generally take longer to dry than when you use an existing mould such as a balloon or bowl.

▲ Pressing a sealed mask into plaster/gypsum

▶ Filling the mould with pulp

■ HOW TO MAKE A CARDBOARD BOX

The basic technique described below can be adapted and expanded to build boxes with coffered or pointed lids, a dolls' house or even an open-fronted skyscraper for storing cassette tapes – the sky's the limit. (You could, of course, take a short cut by using a ready-made cardboard box, such as a shoe box, but remember that the water in wallpaper paste will warp thin card or cardboard.)

EQUIPMENT AND MATERIALS

Sheet of corrugated
  cardboard (size to suit
  your requirements)
Pencil or felt-tip pen
Ruler
Craft knife and scissors
Masking tape

Newspapers
Bowl of wallpaper paste or
  PVA/white glue if
  cardboard is thin
White emulsion paint
  (sealer)
Brush

METHOD Mark out on the cardboard four rectangles of equal dimensions and two squares of equal size, and cut them out using a craft knife or scissors.

▲ **Applying the first layer of paper**

◀ **Covering inside the lid with paper**

Using masking tape, attach three of the rectangles and the two squares to each other so that you have an open box. Ensure that the sides and corners are true.

Cover this structure inside and out with three or more layers of pasted paper pieces (see page 13), taking care not to make the corners bulky – mitre them, if necessary.

Now for the lid. From the spare cardboard cut two rectangles which are about 1–2cm (½–¾in) smaller than the already-cut fourth rectangle (see paragraph one above). Check that these two new rectangles will fit easily inside the box – remember to allow sufficient space for the three or more layers of pasted paper with which you are going to cover the lid.

Tape the two small rectangles one on top of the other and glue or tape them to the centre of the larger rectangle. Then cover the whole neatly with three layers of pasted paper strips. Again, take care over the corners.

Allow both the lid and body of the box to dry thoroughly before sealing them with a layer of white emulsion paint.

Effective methods of decoration include covering the box with handmade or bought paper (see Maureen Hamilton-Hill's work on page 54); glueing on swirls of coarse string or twisted tissue paper (see Nicola Sargent's boxes on page 46) which you then paper or paint over; adding moulded shapes of paper pulp such as bobbles or animal-handles attached by glue and/or masking tape . . . The alternatives are endless, as are the shapes of boxes you can create – circular, heart-shaped, oval, or whatever.

■ HOW TO MAKE A CHICKENWIRE ARMATURE

Using chickenwire as a skeleton, you can create paper objects of almost any size. For a large sculpture, where the chickenwire will have to bear a substantial weight of paper, the structure can be strengthened by creating a wooden frame to support key parts of the armature. If you are going to use pulp, cover the chickenwire first with a layer of pasted pieces of newspaper to help support the pulp. Below we demonstrate how a pig is made using a chickenwire armature.

EQUIPMENT AND MATERIALS

Pliable fine-gauge chicken-wire	Fine sandpaper/glasspaper
Wire-cutters/tin-snips	Scissors
Pair of pliers	String
Newspapers, pink and white	Brushes
	White emulsion paint
Bowl of wallpaper paste	Pencil
Coarse dressmaking pin	Poster paints or similar
PVA/white glue	Matt varnish

METHOD From a roll of chickenwire cut a piece sufficiently large to bend into an oval for the body. Tuck away any spiky ends inside the shape using pliers.

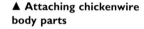

▲ Attaching chickenwire body parts

◄ Pasting on the second layer of paper

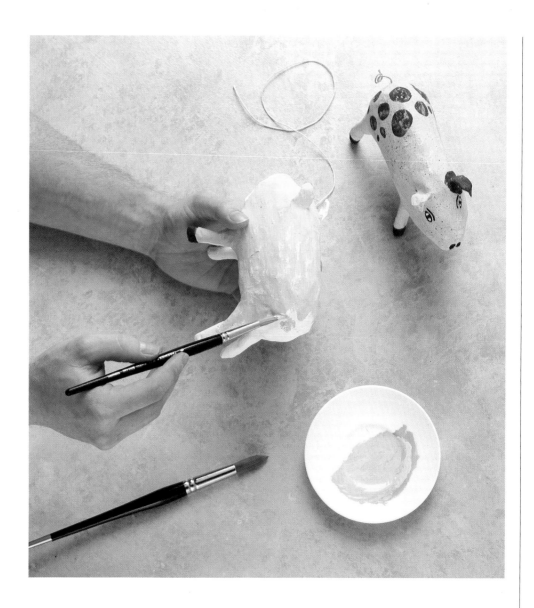

Cover the whole body with four layers of pasted pieces of newspaper and set aside to dry.

For the legs cut four strips of chickenwire and roll them into tubes. Push one end of each into the body where appropriate, adjust the shape of the legs and secure them to the body with small strips of pasted newspaper wrapped round the junction. Twine more pasted strips round and down the legs, then trim the length of the legs with wire-cutters/tin-snips so that the pig stands evenly. Use tiny pieces of pasted paper to mould miniature hooves and leave to dry.

Cut two small spade shapes of chickenwire (i.e. two circles of wire with one protruding spike each) and hold them on the head to check that the shape and proportions are correct for ears. Bend the wire as necessary. Do not forget that a pig's ears curve slightly towards the front. Cover the wire with one layer of pasted paper.

Insert the spike of wire on the ear into the head by piercing a hole in the head with a big needle and pushing the ear spike into it with a blob of PVA/white glue. Then attach both ears firmly with several layers of tiny pasted paper strips.

When the entire pig is dry, smooth any rough patches with fine sandpaper/glasspaper. To create a tail, paint a short length of string with white emulsion and wrap it round a small pencil to dry curly. Make a hole in the rear body with a large needle and insert one end of the tail together with a blob of PVA/white glue.

Then brush on a coat of white emulsion before painting the pig in a mixture of white emulsion with pink and yellow poster paints. When the paint is dry, give the pig's skin texture by rubbing it with coarse sandpaper/glasspaper. Lastly give the pig a protective coat of matt varnish.

▲ Moulding pulp for earrings

▲ Attaching 'fish hooks'

▲ Brushing on a coat of gesso before decorating

■ HOW TO MAKE EARRINGS

EQUIPMENT AND MATERIALS

Scallop shell or mould

Modelling clay

Plaster of Paris/gypsum

Mixing bowl

Materials and equipment
for making paper pulp
(see page 25)

Petroleum jelly

PVA/white glue

Fastenings ('fish
hooks'/clips, etc)

Craft knife/scalpel

Acrylic gesso or materials
and equipment for
making traditional gesso
(see page 36)

Brushes

Gouache paints, etc, to
decorate

Varnish

METHOD The simplest method is to shape pulp directly into a scallop shell mould (see below). Alternatively you can impress part of a small scallop shell into modelling clay and make one or more moulds using plaster of Paris/gypsum (see page 27). A third alternative is to cut cardboard to the same scallop shape and then, with your fingers or a small palette knife, form the pulp on top of the card; but this is a more time-consuming method, especially if you wish to make several pairs of earrings.

To make finely textured pulp, shred good quality paper, e.g. typing paper. Soak it, boil it, liquidize it and then push it through a fine sieve. Squeeze most of the water out of the paper before stirring in ready-mixed wallpaper paste and linseed oil. (Quantities will vary, but, as a rough guide, add two tablespoons of linseed oil to a small washing-up bowl of mashed paper and paste.) Mix thoroughly. Add filler as necessary until the pulp is mouldable – dryish but sticky.

Cover the scallop mould with petroleum jelly, remove any excess and then press the pulp into the mould(s). Leave to dry.

To make round beads roll small quantities of pulp between the palms of your hands until they are evenly shaped. Leave to dry.

To insert 'fish hooks' for pierced ears and tiny metal loops for suspending beads, etc., delicately make an appropriate sized hole with a craft knife or scalpel in the scallop or bead and fix the metal attachments in place with PVA/white glue.

Using a brush, cover the scallops, beads, etc, with three thin layers of gesso (see page 36), allowing for each layer to dry before applying the next. For decorating ideas see pages 75–81 and opposite.

▶ The finished earrings (Julie Howells)

■ HOW TO MAKE YOUR OWN PAPER

Apart from the cost of buying handmade paper in quantity, the chief advantage of making your own is that you can create a wide range of thicknesses, patterns and textures. Remember that the better the quality of paper you use for the pulp, the better the resulting sheets will be.

EQUIPMENT AND MATERIALS

4 or more sheets A2-size coloured paper

Mixing bowl

Water

Large saucepan

Liquidizer/blender

Kitchen sink, deep household decorator's paint tray or deep garden seed tray

1 or more sheets of wire mesh (same gauge as a

sieve) cut to the size you require

Kitchen sink draining board

10 sheets of felt (same size as wire mesh sheet) or disposable cellulose cleaning cloths plus lots of newspaper

2 drawing boards

Clamps (optional)

▲ Lifting wire mesh with pulp

METHOD Tear the paper into pieces about 2.5cm (1in) square. Place in a mixing bowl, cover in water and leave to soak overnight. Drain off the surplus water, put the paper in a saucepan with 2litres (3¼ pints) of water and boil for twenty minutes. Leave to cool, then liquidize/blend into pulp.

Fill the kitchen sink or a deep tray with water, place the wire mesh sheet in the bottom and pour in the paper pulp. The more pulp you add the thicker your sheets of paper will be. Interesting results can be achieved by mixing two or more different coloured pulps – black and white are effective, for example – or by the addition of pressed flowers, pieces of fern, leaves, strands of sparkling material, etc. Stir the pulp and any additional material – the pulp will rise to the surface.

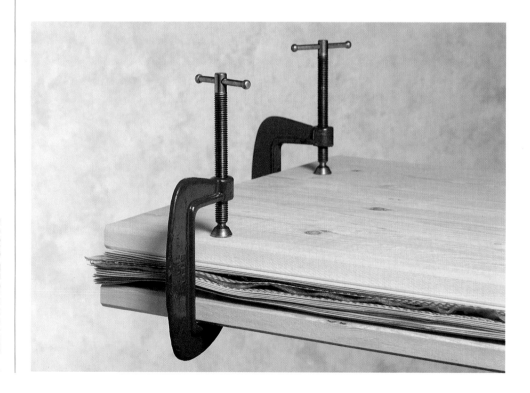

◀ Pressing sheets of pulp in a clamp

▶ Carol Hill's handmade flat panels or sheets are composed on wire mesh from several colours of dyed pulp which bleed more or less into each other. In simple clip frames they make attractive pictures

As you lift the wire mesh out of the water, it will trap a layer of pulp. Lay the mesh on the sink draining board and cover the pulp with either five sheets of felt or with a disposable cellulose cleaning cloth plus a large amount of newspaper interspersed with a couple more cloths.

Turn this 'sandwich' upside down and place it on top of a drawing board on a flat surface. Remove the mesh and, on top of the sheet of pulp, place either five sheets of felt or a disposable cellulose cleaning cloth plus a thick layer of newspaper and more cloths. On top of that place another drawing board.

Clamp the whole stack as tightly as possible to remove all the water or else stand on top of the pile until no more water trickles out.

Separate the stack and lay the sheet of paper pulp out to dry on a flat sheet of mesh, preferably supported beneath to allow air to circulate.

■ HOW TO SEAL AN OBJECT WITH GESSO

You can make your own traditional gesso as described below or acrylic gesso can be purchased in liquid form ready made. After using gesso, soak brushes in warm water immediately afterwards for ten minutes or so and then wash them in soapy water and dry them thoroughly. When gesso dries, it becomes hard, which strengthens a paper object, but does not mean it is unbreakable – it can crack or chip like porcelain. However, when sanded down, gesso also creates a smooth painting surface.

▲ Applying the first coat of gesso

▲ Smoothing out imperfections

Warning: the type of gesso described below may flake if applied to an object containing a lot of PVA/white glue; for such objects acrylic gesso is recommended.

EQUIPMENT AND MATERIALS

Completed paper object
Rabbit-skin glue powder or granules
Water
Mixing bowl
Double saucepan or large saucepan with heat-resistant bowl standing inside
Ground chalk/whiting
Wooden stirring implement
Powdered tempera paint or cotton fabric dye (optional – for colouring gesso – add it with ground chalk/whiting)
Sieve
Brush
Fine and medium sandpaper/glasspaper
Small wooden block (to wrap sandpaper/glasspaper around)

METHOD Mix ⅓ teacup rabbit-skin glue powder with approx 450ml (¾ pint) of boiling water in a bowl. If you are using granules, leave them to soak in the bowl overnight. This mixture is known as rabbit-skin size.

Pour water into the double saucepan or large saucepan, and bring near to boiling point. Pour the rabbit-skin size into the inner container – do not allow the size to boil.

Add 225g (8oz) ground chalk/whiting and stir until the mixture is the consistency of double cream. Sieve out any lumps. As the mixture cools it becomes thicker, so keep it warm. Remove any skin that forms and stir in some more hot water to thin.

Paint the gesso on the paper object both inside and out, making sure any crevices are covered. Many makers prefer to apply several thin layers of gesso as this gives a finer, smoother finish. Allow the final layer of gesso to dry before sanding it with medium and then fine sandpaper.

If any cracks appear, apply another coat of gesso to the damaged area and sand it smooth.

▶ Clock sealed with gesso (Juliette Pearce)

Overleaf: Vases, box and candlestick (Nicola Sargent)

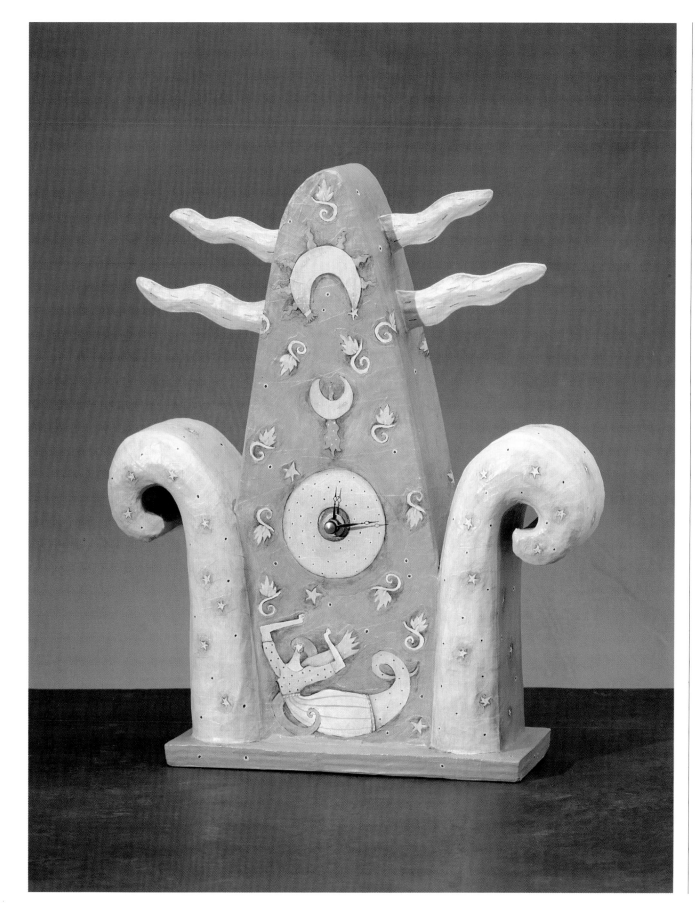

PROJECTS

·VESSELS·

CAROLINE GIBBS

Metallic bowls and dishes

EQUIPMENT AND MATERIALS

Bowls, dishes, etc, as moulds	Brushes
Rabbit-skin glue granules	Equipment and materials for making gesso (see page 36)
Mixing bowl	
Water	Fine sandpaper/glasspaper
Double saucepan or large saucepan with heat-resistant bowl inside	Bole (powdered clay), various colours
Plastic wrap/saran wrap or petroleum jelly	Transfer metal leaf – silver, gold, etc
Masking tape	Goldsize (oil-based varnish)
Newspapers	Fine wire wool (optional)

METHOD Make a fairly strong mix of rabbit-skin glue granules and water in a bowl and leave it to soak overnight. Next day heat a double saucepan of water near to boiling point and pour the size into the inner pan; keep it warm, but do not let the size boil.

Cover the outside of a large bowl or dish with petroleum jelly or with plastic wrap/saran wrap secured by masking tape, and stand it upside down. Tear some newspapers into pieces about 2.5cm (1in) square and dampen them with water (no glue) before applying the first layer to the mould.

To build up the second, third and fourth layers of paper apply the warm rabbit-skin size with a brush to each piece of paper in order to glue it in place. Add further layers if you wish.

When the layers of paper are dry, remove the object from the mould. Make a quantity of traditional gesso (see page 36), checking that there are no air bubbles in it. (Do not use acrylic gesso as this may flake.) With a brush apply six or more thin layers of gesso inside and out. (The water in the gesso will penetrate the paper bowl and distort it to give a crinkled, battered look.)

When dry, carefully smooth the surface of the final layer with fine sandpaper/glasspaper, paying particular attention to the rim, where extra gesso will have gathered because the bowl is upside down.

Paint on three thin coats of bole in the shade of your choice, allowing each layer to dry before applying the next. This provides a good base on which to gild.

Then gild the object with one or more layers of leaf in the colour of your choice. Double gild to achieve opacity, and burnish the leaf with wire wool if you want it to shine. Remember, too, that an attractive finish is created by oxidizing silver leaf. (If you are interested in this rather specialist art, why not read an authoritative book on gilding or take a course in water gilding?)

Finally protect the object with a coat of varnish.

Bowls with a textured surface

EQUIPMENT AND MATERIALS

100g (4oz) coloured paper
  (not newspaper or
  magazines)
Saucepan
Water
Liquidizer/blender
25g (1oz) PVA/white glue
Bowl for mixing
Bowl(s) as mould(s)
Plastic wrap/saran wrap
Masking tape
Fragments of material
  (optional) – silk, foil,
  muslin, etc

Disposable cellulose
  cleaning cloths
Newspapers
Metallic acrylic paints/
  ordinary acrylic
  paints/coloured metallic
  powder paints/non-
  tarnishing wax gilt (as for
  picture frames)/metallic
  oil pastels/gold leaf and
  water-based gold size,
  etc
Brushes
Matt varnish

METHOD Tear the paper into small pieces, soak it for a while in warm water and then boil it, before blending it into a fairly fine pulp. Pour the pulp into a bowl and drain off the surface water. Mix in the PVA/white glue.

Line the inside of the mould with plastic wrap/saran wrap secured in position with masking tape. Press dampened fragments of fabric, if desired, randomly round the interior. Then firmly press handfuls of pulp on top of the fragments and around the inside of the mould. To dry the pulp and compact it effectively roll a cleaning cloth into a ball and press it firmly against the pulp. Repeat this process until the pulp is dryish and stable.

Round the rim pinch the pulp between forefinger and thumb if you wish to create a frilly edge.

If you wish to make several small bowls from a single mould, the damp pulp bowl can be removed from the mould by holding the plastic wrap/saran wrap and gently lifting it out. Carefully remove the wrap and leave the pulp bowl on top of a thick layer of newspapers to dry for several days in a warm place.

Once thoroughly dry, use the paints, etc, suggested above to decorate the bowl, highlighting the texture of the pulp to create an antique look. Seal the bowl with matt varnish.

CAROL HILL

Footed fish bowls and vases

EQUIPMENT AND MATERIALS

Bowls as moulds – I large, I small	PVA/white glue
Balloons as moulds	White emulsion paint
Petroleum jelly	Brushes
Newspapers, etc	Materials and equipment for making gesso (see page 36)
Bowl of wallpaper paste	
Craft knife	Gouache or acrylic paints
Cardboard	Semi-gloss water-based varnish
Masking tape	

METHOD Bowls first. Cover the insides of both bowls with petroleum jelly. Over the inside of the larger bowl mould pasted paper strips (see page 13) – Louise Pearson builds up at least eight layers in one sitting, leaving the paper to stand proud of the rim by about 2.5cm (1in). While the paper is still damp and malleable, roll it over to form the basis of the rounded lip.

Once that is dry, paste thinner, smaller strips over the rim until you achieve the desired thickness.

Cover the inside of the smaller bowl with eight layers of pasted paper pieces and, when dry, trim the rim neatly with scissors or a craft knife (see page 18). Then, following the method on page 19, add a flat cardboard rim. Leave to dry.

Glue the bottom of the small bowl to the bottom of the big bowl, and fill the join with small rolls of pasted paper. The raised decorative motifs are cut from cardboard, pasted in place and then built up by pasting five layers of paper pieces over them. Once all is dry, paint the footed bowl with white emulsion, repair any cracks or holes with gesso, emulsion over those repairs and then decorate with gouache or acrylic paints. Seal with three coats of water-based varnish, allowing each coat to dry before applying the next.

Now for the vase. Following the methods described on page 17, mould eight layers of pasted paper pieces on to a large balloon right up to the neck. The flat base is made by cutting a hole in the bottom of the dried paper balloon and filling this with a circle of cardboard, as described on page 21, method 4. Make a series of vertical cuts round the neck of the vase and splay out the paper, dampening it slightly first, if necessary. Paste small paper strips first horizontally round and then vertically over the rim until the desired shape is achieved. As decorative features thin paper rolls are stuck on in twirly shapes with PVA/white glue and masking tape. Then emulsion, repair, decorate and seal in the same manner as the footed bowl.

Boxes

EQUIPMENT AND MATERIALS

Planks of wood	Waterproof acrylic black
Handsaw	ink
Hammer and nails	Brushes
Tissue paper	Watercolour paints
Bowl of wallpaper paste	Matt cellulose lacquer
Pair of metal hinges and	spray
pins	

METHOD Make a wooden box, but do not yet attach the lid. Cover it inside and out – the lid as well – with as many layers as you like of pasted tissue paper pieces until the wood is invisible. To add texture wrinkle the paper or, as Nicola Sargent has done on one of her boxes, paste on snaking rolls of paper to the top of the lid and sides.

Affix the metal hinges to the box and lid, then decorate with ink and watercolours before applying several layers of protective sealant.

NICOLA SARGENT

Blue bowl

EQUIPMENT AND MATERIALS

Large bowl as mould

Plastic wrap/saran wrap

Masking tape

Newspapers, etc

Bowl of wallpaper paste

Materials and equipment
  for making gesso (see
  page 36)

Brushes

Fine sandpaper/glasspaper

Incising tool

Blue bole (powdered clay)

Blue oil paint

Gold transfer leaf

Fine wire wool

Matt cellulose lacquer
  spray

METHOD Using the method described on page 13, mould ten layers of pasted paper pieces on the inside of a large bowl. When the paper is dry, apply twenty thin layers of gesso, sanding each dry layer smooth before applying the next.

With an incising tool, inscribe the pattern of your choice in the gesso.

Paint the whole bowl with two coats of bole and sand them off patchily when dry. Emphasize the incised pattern with blue oil paint. Once this is dry, apply one or more layers of gold leaf, as desired. When dry, burnish the leaf with thin wire wool before sealing with varnish.

Tubular pot

EQUIPMENT AND MATERIALS

Flexible smooth cardboard
  or card
Scissors
Masking tape
Newspapers, etc
Bowl of wallpaper paste
Materials and equipment
  for making gesso (see
  page 36)

Brushes
Waterproof Indian ink
Gouache paints
Semi-gloss cellulose
  lacquer spray

METHOD Cut a length of cardboard or card and roll it into a tube. Tape it firmly in shape. Cut a circle of cardboard or card to fit snugly inside one end of the tube and tape it in place.

Cover the pot inside and out with at least five layers of pasted paper pieces, taking care to make the rim as smooth as possible.

Once the paper pot is dry, four layers of gesso are applied. Allow time for each coat to dry before applying the next – it does not take long.

Nicola Sargent then draws on the outline of her pattern in waterproof ink and fills it in with gouache colours, before finally covering the pot with several layers of protective lacquer.

For fresh flowers, insert a glass or plastic container inside the pot to protect papier mâché from water

Hanging pot

EQUIPMENT AND MATERIALS

Balloon as mould	Brushes
Newspapers, etc	Incising tool
Bowl of wallpaper paste	Silver transfer leaf
Scissors and craft knife	Acrylic waterproof black ink
Materials and equipment for making gesso (see page 36)	Semi-gloss lacquer spray
	Chains and hooks

METHOD Following the method described on page 17, mould a vase shape on a balloon with at least five layers of pasted paper pieces. Open the neck by making vertical scissor cuts all round. Fan open the paper and strengthen the neck with further horizontal and vertical pasted paper strips until you achieve the shape desired. Leave it to dry.

Using scissors or a craft knife, make three holes near the rim of the pot and tidy the rough edges with paste.

Apply six thin layers of gesso, following the method described on page 36. When the final layer is dry, delicately inscribe a pattern into the gesso with an incising tool. Remove any dust clinging to the vessel and float on one or more layers of silver leaf. After a while, left like this, the leaf will tarnish to the shade of Nicola Sargent's pot.

Acrylic ink is applied to the incised pattern and then the pot is given a protective coat of lacquer. Thread the hooks through the holes round the rim and attach the chains for hanging.

NICOLA SARGENT

Muslin bowls with beads

EQUIPMENT AND MATERIALS

Square and round bowls
  as moulds

Plastic wrap/saran wrap

Masking tape

Muslin or fine cheesecloth

Bowl of wallpaper paste

Newspapers, etc

Scissors or scalpel

White emulsion paint

Brushes

Gloss yacht varnish

For square bowl:

Acrylic and gold paints

Glass 'gemstones' with flat
  backs

PVA/white glue

For gold bowl:

Gold, black and purple
  acrylic paints

Coarse needle and black
  silk string

16 black and 8 white
  wooden beads

8 plastic mirror 'scimitars'

For striped bowl:

Orange and peacock blue
  acrylic paints

Coarse needle and black
  silk string

8 matt black, 8 faceted
  'jet' and 8 natural wood
  beads

METHOD All three bowls are created using the same basic methods. Cover the inside of the mould with plastic wrap/saran wrap secured by masking tape. Dip a piece of muslin in the wallpaper paste and line the mould with it. Apply four or more layers of pasted paper pieces and, for the two round bowls, apply a final layer of pasted muslin. In the case of the square bowl, let the layers protrude above the rim of the mould to form rough points.

With scissors or a scalpel, trim the rims of the round bowls neatly (see page 18). Trim the rim of the square bowl into spikes if necessary. Coat all three bowls with white emulsion and leave to dry.

Decorate the square bowl in shades of orange, peacock and gold, outline the rim in black and, when dry, affix the glass stones to the inside with PVA/white glue. Apply a coat of yacht varnish.

For the gold bowl, paint on a layer of gold paint and patterns in black and purple. Make eight small holes round the rim with a scalpel. Coat it with yacht varnish. Using eight lengths of silk string, tie a knot in one end of each, thread on two black beads, one white one and a 'scimitar'. Thread a needle with the string through into the inside of the bowl, round the lip and back to the outside, where the loose end is neatly knotted.

The striped bowl is painted orange and blue, and again eight holes are made round the rim. Apply a coat of yacht varnish. Each of the pieces of silk string is knotted at one end, has three beads put on it and the loose end knotted inside the bowl.

Vases

EQUIPMENT AND MATERIALS

Bottles, rectangular ridged vase, and circular dish as moulds

Plastic wrap/saran wrap

Masking tape

Handmade paper (see page 34) or high-quality coloured paper

Bowl of wallpaper paste

Brush

Spirit-based paper varnish

Spray can of water repellant

Flexible metal flange as stand

METHOD For the two vases on the left, cover a bottle as smoothly as possible with plastic wrap/saran wrap secured by masking tape. Dampen a sheet of handmade paper or coloured paper. Maureen Hamilton-Hill intentionally makes her paper with holes in it, but irregularly shaped holes can be torn in damp paper. Wrap the damp paper round the side and base of the bottle, and brush wallpaper paste on to the areas of paper which overlap. Smooth the joins, particularly on the base. When dry, coat the paper inside and out with varnish and give it a final coat of water repellant for added protection.

The rectangular pot is moulded on the outside of a vase with ridged sides. Because the outline would be blurred by plastic wrap/saran wrap, the first layer of handmade paper pieces to be applied is merely dampened, not pasted. At the sides the paper is pinched together to form a projecting seam. Two subsequent layers are affixed with wallpaper paste and left to dry.

To remove the paper vase from the mould cut down through the centre of the side seams and across the base with a scalpel. Immediately rejoin the two halves with wallpaper paste and cover the join in the base with small pieces of pasted paper. The dry vase is then sprayed with water repellant before being given a coat of varnish.

The right-hand vase is moulded in two halves on a circular ceramic dish. Once again the first layer is of damp, unpasted paper pieces extending beyond the mould to form a rim, but not covering the whole dish. Two pasted layers of paper pieces are then added. Repeat the process for the second half. When the two duplicate dishes are dry, paste them together, leaving a small unpasted gap at the bottom, where a piece of flanged flexible metal is inserted to form a stand. A coating of water repellant and a coat of varnish complete the process.

MAUREEN HAMILTON-HILL

Golden boxes

EQUIPMENT AND MATERIALS

Mounting board or any good card

PVA/white glue

Typing paper/newspaper/ brown wrapping paper (if handmade paper is thin)

Materials and equipment for making paper (see page 34) or shop-bought handmade paper

Bowl of wallpaper paste

Water repellant sealer

Brush

Spirit-based paper varnish or semi-gloss household interior varnish

METHOD Maureen Hamilton-Hill uses techniques similar to those described on page 28, but, instead of cardboard, she prefers to use mounting card and attaches the pieces of the box with adhesive only – no tape as it is too coarse for her work.

To achieve a speckled look, she applies acrylic paints or fabric dyes to plain paper before making pulp for her handmade paper.

If the handmade paper is thin, apply a pasted layer of typing paper, newspaper or brown wrapping paper first, taking particular care over the corners.

Finally the box should be given a waterproof coating and, when that is dry, a coat of matt or semi-gloss varnish.

For a paperweight, cover large pebbles from the beach with a layer of pasted handmade paper sealed with varnish

MAUREEN HAMILTON-HILL

VESSELS

Découpage bowls

EQUIPMENT AND MATERIALS

Bowls or woks as moulds
Newspapers
Bowl of wallpaper paste
PVA/white glue
Brush
Materials and equipment
   for making paper from
   coloured pulp (see page
   25) or shop-bought
   handmade paper in
   various colours
Pencil
Scalpel or scissors
Sheet of fine card
   (optional)
Semi-gloss varnish

METHOD On the inside of a bowl or wok apply a layer of damp, unpasted pieces of newspaper reaching up to, but not over, the rim. Apply five layers of pasted pieces of newspaper, taking care to keep the rim as neat and even as possible. Set aside to dry for several days.

To prevent warping, remove the paper bowl from its mould and paint it all over with a coat of diluted PVA/white glue. Leave to dry.

On a selection of different coloured sheets of hand-made paper – Gerry Copp makes her own and gives it texture by pressing the pulp between disposable cellulose cleaning cloths – draw simple flowers and shapes. Cut out a card pattern of each design, if you wish, so that the shapes can be replicated swiftly in quantity. Cut out the paper shapes and paste them in overlapping layers on both faces of the bowl. Take care to smooth the rim and remember to decorate the base as well once the rim is dry.

When the bowl is completely dry, cover it with two coats of semi-gloss varnish.

GERRY COPP

Rose bowls

EQUIPMENT AND MATERIALS

Bowl as a mould	Wrapping paper or
Plastic wrap/saran wrap	wallpaper
Masking tape	Bowl of wallpaper paste
Materials and equipment	Gouache paints
for making pulp (see	Gold paint, wax crayons
page 25)	or oil pastels
Disposable cellulose	Oil glaze
cleaning cloths	Semi-gloss varnish
White emulsion paint	Jigsaw
Brushes	Fine sandpaper/glasspaper

METHOD It is perfectly feasible to make these bowls by layering pasted paper on an existing mould (see page 13) and then cut out the rim with scissors or a scalpel. This is, however, a lengthy process, if you wish to make a thick bowl, and trimming the edge can be tricky. For these reasons Rosy Burman and Kathy Webster of Paper Roses prefer to work on bowls made of pulp.

Begin by making an appropriate quantity of paper pulp using PVA/white glue instead of any wallpaper paste, and fine sawdust as a filler instead of ground chalk/whiting (see page 25).

Mould the pulp over the inside of a bowl that is slightly larger than the size of paper bowl you wish to make, following the directions given on page 13. Compact the pulp as densely as possible with the aid of a smooth wad of disposable cellulose cleaning cloth and set aside to dry. Paint the paper bowl inside and out with white emulsion.

From floral paper tear largish pieces depicting roses and foliage; paste these on, overlapping one slightly with another, working from the rim downwards. When this layer is dry, if you wish, paint on an intermittent band of fake ribbon in gouache.

Paint the outside in two coats of rusty red gouache and emphasize the pulp's texture by lightly brushing on dryish gold paint or by rubbing it with gold wax crayons or oil pastels.

On the inside apply a coat of oil glaze. Due to the fact that it is most thoroughly absorbed by the torn paper edges, this brings out the three-dimensional quality of the work and softens the bright colours.

When that is dry, coat the whole vessel with one or more layers of varnish, before cutting round the edge of the flowers and leaves on the rim with a jigsaw. Smooth any rough patches with sandpaper and then paint the raw edge with one or more layers of gold paint. Finally seal that with varnish.

Tall vases

EQUIPMENT AND MATERIALS

Large balloon as mould	Fine sandpaper/glasspaper
Newspapers, etc	White emulsion paint
Bowl of wallpaper paste	Brushes
Flexible cardboard or card	Gouache paints
Scissors or craft knife	Semi-gloss varnish
Masking tape	

METHOD The larger of Juliette Pearce's two vases is over 1.2m (4ft) high. Mould five layers of pasted paper pieces over a large balloon (see page 17). When dry, make numerous vertical scissor cuts into both ends of the paper balloon shape and splay out the paper. From cardboard or card fashion two loose conical shapes and slip the broad end of each into the two holes in the paper vessel. Adjust the shapes carefully before taping them in place. Then add a splayed cardboard neck (see page 20) to each end for a base and finished neck. Cut out and affix a circle of cardboard to fill the base.

Cover the whole vessel inside (as far as possible) and out with up to seven layers of pasted paper pieces. Smooth the surface with fine sandpaper/glasspaper.

After a coat of emulsion, decorate the vase in gouache paints. When dry, apply several coats of protective varnish.

Winged bowl

EQUIPMENT AND MATERIALS

Bowl as a mould	Masking tape
Newspapers	White emulsion paint
Bowl of wallpaper paste	Brushes
Smooth cardboard	Acrylic paints
Pencil or felt pen	Semi-gloss varnish
Scissors or craft knife	

METHOD Tear the newspaper into small pieces and follow the directions on page 13 for layering paper on the inside of an existing mould – in this case the bowl. Up to eight layers of pasted paper pieces will be necessary. Leave to dry.

Draw the wings freehand on cardboard, cut them out, tape them to the sides of the paper bowl and then cover them with three layers of pasted paper pieces.

Once dry, coat the whole vessel with white emulsion before decorating. Juliette Pearce uses acrylic paints freehand, but you could colour black-and-white photocopies. Her bowl is protected with two layers of varnish.

Stitched vessels and box of memories

EQUIPMENT AND MATERIALS

Large planters as moulds	**Bowl of wallpaper paste**
Chickenwire	**Brown wrapping paper**
Wire-cutters/tin-snips	**Scalpel**
Coarse string	**Sewing needle and thread**
Scissors	**PVA/white glue**
Pair of pliers	**Small sponge**
Polythene or plastic	**Large gourd as a mould**
sheeting	**Silk thread**
Masking tape	**Recycled copper-coated**
Materials and equipment	**thread**
for making paper (see	**Metallic powder paints**
page 34)	**Brushes**

METHOD The basis for the lower half of the two large pots, each of which is about 60cm (21in) high, is a terracotta planter. Because this is not tall enough, chickenwire is tied with string to the rim, extending upwards, and this is bent into the desired form. Tuck away spiky ends with pliers. Cover the mould with polythene or plastic sheeting secured with masking tape.

Using wallpaper paste, cover the outside of the mould with pieces of handmade paper and then add several layers of pasted brown paper pieces. The final layer is again of handmade paper. Leave it to dry.

To remove the mould, use a scalpel to cut the paper vessel horizontally in half at its widest point. Since glue is not strong enough, the two halves are stitched together with a needle and coarse thread. The join is then disguised by pasting on pieces of handmade paper.

The raised patterns on both the larger vessels are made from coarse string and rolls of newspaper glued on and covered in a layer of pasted pieces of handmade paper. When that is dry, a coating of diluted PVA/white glue is sponged on and allowed to dry before dye and metallic powders are dusted on.

The bowl is made of one single layer of pasted handmade paper pieces moulded on a gourd. Since the gourd cannot be removed without splitting the paper, this may be regarded as a bonus, providing the opportunity to repair the splits with stitching in silk and copper-coated threads retrieved from old electric flex. A coating of diluted PVA/white glue is applied before the bowl is dusted with metallic powders.

Cas Holmes's box contains memorabilia from a special day at the seaside. Found lidless on the beach, the box lid is made from cardboard and that day's newspaper. Why not adapt this idea to mark a special occasion of your own?

CAS HOLMES

Vase and jug with pleated necks, and seahorse vase

EQUIPMENT AND MATERIALS

For vase and jug:

Handmade or good quality paper

Bowl of wallpaper paste

Plastic or paper bag (as mould)

For seahorse vase:

Materials and equipment for making pulp (see p.25)

Cold-water material dye

Balloon

Box of coarse sand (optional)

PVA/white glue

Gold and metallic paints

Matt varnish

Brush

METHOD The vase and jug with pleated necks are both made from Miriam Troth's own handmade paper, which is fairly thick. For the main body of both, large pieces of pasted paper were moulded round a malleable, air-filled bag. A strip of paper folded into pleats was pasted to the necks of both vessels and, in the case of the jug, simply extended downwards while damp to form a handle.

The conical body of the seahorse vase began as dyed pulp moulded on to part of a balloon, with extra pulp added to form the pointed end. The seahorses and starfish, which are rounded on both sides, are shaped by hand – Miriam Troth uses a box of sand to hold them while they dry, but they could be made in two halves and glued together (see page 27).

After lengthy drying, the pieces are secured to the main vessel with PVA/white glue. Metallic paints are then smeared on the dyed pulp with fingers or a brush.

Finally all three vessels are sealed with a matt varnish.

MIRIAM TROTH

Giant dish and Ali Baba jar

EQUIPMENT AND MATERIALS

Pair of protective gloves

Coarse-gauge chickenwire

Wire-cutters/tin-snips

Pair of pliers

Newspapers

Bowl of wallpaper paste

Pliable cardboard

PVA/white glue

Masking tape

Scissors

Sand (optional)

Wall-lining paper

White emulsion paint

Acrylic paints, wax
   crayons, waterproof
   black ink

Brushes

Matt paper varnish

METHOD The huge dish is formed from a large circle of chickenwire with the rim turned in and the spiky ends tucked away using a pair of pliers. Bend the wire into a concave shape and cover both sides with six or more layers of pasted pieces of newspaper. As a final layer apply large pasted pieces of wall-lining paper to create a smooth painting surface.

Coat the dish with emulsion and, when dry, decorate in acrylics and crayons, outling the pattern in waterproof ink. Finally apply a coat of paper varnish to prevent discolouration.

The basis of the jar is also chickenwire. Its round main body is comprised of two pieces, each carefully cut to the shape of Mercator's flat projection of the Earth as shown in an atlas, i.e. virtually straight at top and bottom, but strongly curved on either side. Using the spiky raw edges, these two pieces are carefully joined together. A circle of chicken wire forms a base.

Before attaching a circle of chickenwire for the neck, cover the inside of the jar with at least five layers of pasted newspaper and a final layer of wall-lining paper. To weight the base and stabilize the jar, put a fair quantity of sand between one or more of the layers covering the inside of the base.

Attach the wire neck and cover it with three layers of pasted newspaper pieces. To create a rounded lip, attach a roll of newspaper to the outer rim, secure it in place with masking tape and cover it with at least two layers of paper. When the whole jar is covered in at least five layers of newspaper pieces and is dry, attach two cardboard handles with PVA/white glue and masking tape. Cover the rest of the jar and handles with a layer of pasted wall-lining paper. Coat the jar with emulsion and then decorate as before. Seal with a coat of matt paper varnish.

MALCOLM TEMPLE

Vessels with stalks, leaves and letters

EQUIPMENT AND MATERIALS

Bowls and a dish as moulds

Plastic wrap/saran wrap

Masking tape

Handmade paper (see page 34) or top quality coloured paper

Bowl of wallpaper paste

Dried plant stalks and leaves

Photocopies of letters or letters cut from newspapers

Waterproofer

Spirit-based paper varnish

Brushes

METHOD For translucent vessels Maureen Hamilton-Hill generally uses her own thin handmade paper, which is made solely from pulp and water (see page 34). However, she also sometimes uses coloured paper napkins, pieces of fabric – yellow silk is a favourite – and dried or pressed plant material.

Cover the inside of the mould in plastic wrap/saran wrap affixed with masking tape. Tear handmade paper (several different colours, if you wish) into pieces and dampen it. Paste the pieces and build up three or four layers for smallish vessels, up to six layers for larger vessels. With thin layers the finish is smoother and joins less noticeable – unless, of course, the joins are part of the design.

The bowl on the left features pressed plant stalks inserted between the second and third layers, while for the right-hand bowl pressed leaves were pasted on to the final layer of paper when it was still damp. The dish in the front has photocopied letters pasted on to the top layer and partly over-painted in diluted white emulsion.

Once the vessels are dry, apply a coat of waterproofer and, when that too is dry, seal pale paper objects with paper varnish so that they do not discolour; darker objects may be sealed with household interior quality varnish.

MAUREEN HAMILTON-HILL

Jug with scene inset

EQUIPMENT AND MATERIALS

Large jug as mould	Fine sandpaper/glasspaper
Newspapers	Poster paints or similar
Bowl of wallpaper paste	Matt varnish
Scalpel	Coarse sewing needle
PVA/white glue	Embroidery cotton
Small bowl as mould	*For scene furnishings:*
Pencil	Fine wire
Masking tape	Balsa wood or similar
Gummed paper tape	softwood
String	Tiny found objects or
White emulsion paint	doll's house articles
Brushes	Craft knife

METHOD If you wish, the jug can be moulded on a balloon (see page 17) and then a rim, handle and base may be added (see pages 18, 23 and 20), but Melanie Williams uses a large porcelain jug as a mould. Over the outside, including the handle, a layer of damp, unpasted newspaper pieces is applied instead of a sealer, followed by five or more layers of pasted paper pieces.

When these are dry, carefully slice the paper jug in half vertically – through the handle and avoiding where the scene will be inset.

Glue the two pieces together immediately, before they have time to warp, with PVA/white glue. Secure the join with strips of masking tape. When the glue is dry, carefully remove the masking tape and replace it with gummed paper tape for strength.

Enlarge the spout and rim, if you so wish, with further layers of pasted pieces of newspaper. Neaten the rim by pasting strips of paper over the edge from inside to outside (see page 18) and leave to dry.

Meanwhile, on the inside of a small bowl, build up five or more layers of newspaper pieces, the first layer unpasted so that it will not adhere to the mould. When dry, remove the paper bowl from the mould, hold it against the outside of the paper jug and mark in pencil the outline of the bowl's rim on the jug. With a scalpel cut out a hole and affix the paper bowl in place with PVA/white glue and masking tape. When dry, replace the latter with gummed paper tape. Secure the join with small strips of pasted paper and leave to dry.

Smooth any rough patches with sandpaper/glasspaper before brushing the whole jug with a coat of white emulsion. With a pencil outline your chosen decorative features. The raised letters are formed by pieces of string affixed with glue or paste and then emulsioned. Paint the jug, including the 'walls' and chequered 'floor' of the inset scene.

Melanie's birdcage is fashioned from fine wire, the cupboard shaped with a craft knife from balsa wood, and the vase of flowers from tiny pieces of pasted paper.

The jug is sprayed with matt varnish. Once dry, the rims are blanket stitched, strengthening the structure and providing an original decorative feature.

Attractive raised patterns can be created
by gluing on string of various sizes and textures

MARION ELLIOT

Casket

EQUIPMENT AND MATERIALS

Sheets of smooth-sided corrugated cardboard

Metal ruler

Pencil or felt-tip pen

Craft knife and scissors

PVA/white glue

Masking tape

Gummed paper tape

Newspapers

Bowl of wallpaper paste

Modelling plastic

Petroleum jelly

White emulsion paint

Gouache paints

Waterproof black ink

Brushes

Gloss polyurethane varnish

METHOD Beginning with the base, cut from the cardboard a rectangle 30.5cm × 23cm (12in × 9in), two strips 30.5cm × 6.5cm (12in × 2½in), and two strips 23cm × 6.5cm (9in × 2½in). On one side of each strip cut out simple curves or whatever shape you prefer. Seal both sides of all the pieces with diluted PVA/white glue, and allow it to dry before assembling them.

Apply PVA/white glue to the edges of the large rectangle and to the appropriate edges of the four strips. To keep the pieces in place until the glue dries apply strips of masking tape to each join before gluing the next one. When dry, replace the masking tape with gummed paper tape to strengthen the joins.

For the body of the casket cut two cardboard rectangles 28cm × 12.5cm (11in × 5in), and two 20.5cm × 12.5cm (8in × 5in). Seal all the pieces with a coating of diluted PVA/white glue. When dry, join these four pieces to each other and affix them centrally on top of the base with PVA/white glue and masking tape, replacing the latter by gummed paper tape once the glue is dry.

To create the lid begin by cutting one rectangle of cardboard 29cm × 21.5cm (11½in × 8½in), and two pieces 27.5cm × 20cm (10¾in × 7¾in). Seal all three pieces with diluted PVA/white glue and, when dry, glue the two smaller pieces together, one flat on top of the other (see page 00 on making a box).

Next glue both of these pieces to the centre of the large rectangle. Keep them all in place with masking tape until the glue is completely dry; then replace with gummed paper tape.

For the 'roof' on the lid cut two equilateral triangles of 18cm (7in) and two rectangles 25cm × 5cm (9¾in × 2in). Seal all four pieces with a coat of diluted PVA/white glue and join them together in the manner described above. Then glue and tape the roof centrally on top of the lid.

For the ridge cut a piece of cardboard 25cm × 5cm (9¾in × 2in) and cut a serpentine pattern along one side. Attach the plain side to the ridge with glue and tape as before.

Three layers of pasted paper pieces are then applied over the whole casket, inside and out. Leave to dry for at least two days.

Meanwhile, shape modelling plastic into eighteen balls plus one egg shape and coat them with petroleum jelly. Cover them with five layers of small pasted paper pieces and allow to dry for several days. Then cut them in half, remove the modelling plastic and glue the hemispheres round the base of the box and along the ridge, securing them with masking tape while the glue dries. Remove the masking tape and apply a layer of tiny pasted paper pieces to the joins.

When all is dry, coat the casket inside and out with two layers of white emulsion, allowing time for each to dry.

Draw on your design in pencil and fill in the background colours. Next do the overpainting and, once that is dry, use black ink to add outlines and details. Finally apply three coats of varnish, allowing plenty of drying time between each.

Fish pot with glasses

MATERIALS AND EQUIPMENT

Balloon as mould	Masking tape
Newspapers	Modelling plastic
Bowl of wallpaper paste	White emulsion paint
Cup or small bowl as	Brushes
stand for drying	Poster, acrylic or gouache
Cardboard	paints
Pencil	PVA/white glue
Craft knife	Gloss varnish

METHOD Blow up a balloon until it is pear-shaped and tie a knot in the neck. Then follow the directions on page 17 for layering pasted paper on a balloon. Once the paper layers are dry, burst the balloon and remove it. Cut a hole in what will be the top of the pot and neaten the rim with strips of pasted newspaper.

On a sheet of cardboard draw the two side fins and a tail of appropriate size, and cut them out with a craft knife. Cover all three pieces with at least two layers of pasted newspaper pieces and leave to dry.

From two circles of cardboard create a flat base for the pot, following the directions for method 2 on page 21.

Secure the tail to the open, slightly pointed, end of the paper balloon with masking tape, and cover the join inside and out with several layers of small pasted paper pieces. Affix the fins to either side of the pot with tape and pasted paper pieces.

The fish's features are moulded in modelling plastic straight on to the front of the pot. They are then covered in three or more layers of pasted paper pieces before being left to dry.

From cardboard cut out a simple pair of spectacles of a suitable size to fit behind the side fins. Bend the cardboard to form arms and then cover in two or more layers of pasted paper pieces.

Coat the pot and spectacles with emulsion and, when dry, decorate in the colours of your choice. Glue the spectacles in place. Lastly apply one or more coats of gloss varnish for strength and protection.

AMANDA GODDEN

·JEWELRY·

Chestful of earrings and necklaces

EQUIPMENT AND MATERIALS

Modelling plastic or clay	Coarse sewing needle
Materials and equipment for making plaster moulds (see page 27)	PVA/white glue
	Acrylic gesso
	Brushes
Petroleum jelly	Gold paint or ink, acrylic paints, etc
Materials and equipment for making pulp (see page 25) with typing paper	Matt varnish
	Tiny glass beads
	Thread and clasp for necklace
Sieve	
Earring clips, 'fish-hooks', loops, etc	

METHOD For earrings, mould modelling plastic or clay into shell shapes or impress a tiny scallop shell into a small mound of plastic or clay (see page 27). Coat the mould with petroleum jelly and duplicate the shapes in a tray of plaster of Paris/gypsum (see page 27).

Make a suitable quantity of finely textured pulp from good quality typing paper (see page 25), which is pushed through a sieve before being mixed with the other ingredients. The pulp should be malleable – dryish, but sticky. Cover the plaster moulds with petroleum jelly and then press pulp firmly into them. Leave them to dry for several days.

To insert 'fish-hooks' for pierced ears and metal loops for suspending beads, etc, make holes through the dry pulp with a coarse sewing needle. Affix ear clips with PVA/white glue.

To make beads for necklaces or earrings, patiently mould pulp between the palms of your hands until perfectly round. Once dry, use a coarse needle to pierce a hole through each bead, if you want to thread them into a necklace.

Cover both earrings and beads in three coats of acrylic gesso, allowing each layer to dry before applying the next. (Julie Howells uses acrylic gesso because her pet rabbits, which have the run of her studio, enjoy eating traditional gesso, but will not touch acrylic.)

Apply a layer of gold ink or paint to earrings and beads before using a pointillist technique to paint layer upon layer of tiny coloured dots.

Finally seal the jewelry with a coat of matt varnish and attach miniature decorative beading, if you so wish, with PVA/white glue.

Earrings and brooches

EQUIPMENT AND MATERIALS

Secondhand earrings, *objets trouvés*, etc	Newspapers
Commercial fruit trays of moulded paper pulp	Bowl of wallpaper paste
Craft knife	Metal earclips, 'fish-hooks', brooch pins, etc
Handmade or wrapping paper	Cardboard
PVA/white glue	Coarse sewing needle or scalpel
Acrylic paints	Fine sandpaper/glasspaper
Brushes	Matt or semi-gloss varnish

METHOD Miriam Troth enjoys recycling materials and incorporating *objets trouvés* (often gleaned from car boot sales) in her own creations.

The oval earrings reminiscent of oyster shells are basically made from machine-moulded pulp trays with concave indentations used by fruiterers for transporting apples, etc. Miriam cuts out a pointed oval and covers it with handmade painted paper affixed with PVA/ white glue. She then makes one or two slits lengthways through the concave shape. The areas outside the slits are bent upwards, away from the rest of the earring. The raw cut edges are delicately coloured.

Alternatively the pulp shape may be covered in several layers of small pasted paper pieces, painted in acrylics and then varnished.

Earring clips or 'fish-hooks', or even whole earrings, are then attached by tiny metal links inserted through the paper earrings via a hole made with a coarse sewing needle or scalpel.

Miriam's zig-zag brooches are made of dampened handmade paper pasted on to very damp cardboard, which is then pleated and left to dry before being cut into pieces with a sharp craft knife. A brooch pin is then attached to the back with PVA/white glue.

The rectangular and abstract brooches are of cardboard covered in several layers of paper pieces affixed with PVA/white glue. They are then sanded smooth and decorated in acrylic and metallic paints or are covered in handmade paper before being coated with varnish.

MIRIAM TROTH

Bracelets, earrings and brooch

EQUIPMENT AND MATERIALS

Materials and equipment for making pulp (see page 25)	Scissors
	Silver coins
	Existing cheap earrings and brooches
Crab claws	
PVA/white glue	Metal earring clips, brooch pins and links
Brushes	
White emulsion paint	Flat-backed glass 'jewels'
Powder paints	Matt and gloss varnish
Foil and cellophane sweet wrappers, etc	

METHOD The central bangle above is shaped freehand from paper pulp. While the pulp is damp, real crab claws are inset with PVA/white glue and extra pulp moulded round the bases. When dry, a coat of white emulsion is applied. Powder paints and foil are used to decorate the bangle.

The other bangle, on the left, is made in similar fashion, but with small silver coins inset into pulp instead of claws.

The fish earrings are modelled freehand from pulp. While the pulp is slightly damp, insert a metal 'fish-hook'. When dry, foil and cellophane wrappers are attached with PVA/white glue, with the cellophane twisted and trimmed with scissors into a tail.

The triple-tiered circular earrings are also made from pulp covered in sweet wrappers, but this time moulded on top of an ugly pair of existing earrings.

The 'jewelled' pendant earrings are again modelled freehand from pulp with glass jewels pressed into the damp pulp with a blob of glue. Metal links are also inserted at this stage. When dry, the pulp is painted a dull silver. Finally varnish is applied to the painted areas and metal ear-clips are glued to the backs.

The moon at the top of the brooch is shop bought with a pin already attached and is then covered in a thin layer of pulp. While the pulp is damp, a metal link from which to suspend the lower part of the brooch is inserted and the pulp left to dry. The lower part of the brooch is moulded freehand from pulp with any handy implement. Again the joining link is inserted through the damp pulp. Powder paints and metal foil are used to decorate before sealing with varnish.

Bangles and earrings

EQUIPMENT AND MATERIALS

Pliable cardboard or card	White emulsion paint
Scissors or a craft knife	Pencil or waterproof felt
Masking tape	pen
Newspapers, etc	Acrylic paints
Bowl of wallpaper paste	Waterproof black ink
Materials and equipment	Brushes
for making pulp (see	Gloss varnlsh
page 25)	Metal loops and 'fish-
Fine sandpaper/glasspaper	hooks' (for earrings)

METHOD To make a bangle, cut a strip of card or cardboard approximately 5cm (2 inches) wide and roll it into a circle fixed in place with masking tape. Cover the card or cardboard with at least three layers of pasted paper pieces as smoothly as possible, especially on the inside. Leave to dry.

Make a small quantity of dryish paper pulp and apply this to the outside of the bangle to create a curved outline. When the pulp has dried, go over the outside of the bangle with a piece of fine sandpaper/glasspaper to remove any irregularities.

Paint the bangle with white emulsion and leave to dry.

With a pencil or waterproof pen, draw a pattern on the outside and paint the strongly coloured areas. Use black waterproof ink or black acrylic paint to cover the inside of the bangle, the rims and the outlines. Finally apply two coats of gloss varnish.

The earrings are simply made from cardboard or card shapes, to which wire loops and fish-hooks have been attached before three or more layers of small pasted paper pieces are neatly applied. Once dry, they are decorated and sealed in the same way as the bangle.

Heart, fish and bird brooches

EQUIPMENT AND MATERIALS

Equipment and materials for making plaster moulds (see page 27)

Equipment and materials for making pulp (see page 25)

Petroleum jelly/releasing agent

Palette knife

White emulsion paint

Paint brushes

Gouache paints, various colours

Metallic brooch pins (from craft/art supplies shop)

PVA/white glue

METHOD Following the method described on page 27, make one or more plaster moulds of a heart, a fish or a bird. Then make a quantity of finely textured paper pulp, following the directions given in the recipe on page 25.

Cover the inside of the mould with petroleum jelly or other releasing agent. Press paper pulp firmly into the mould until it is full. Smooth the surface with a palette knife, removing any surplus pulp. Put the full mould in a warm, airy place to dry for several days.

When the paper is completely dry, paint the brooch with white emulsion paint. Decorate with one or two coats of gouache paints in the colours of your choice.

When the decoration is dry, apply a protective coat of varnish. Finally, affix a brooch pin to the back with PVA/white glue.

> *Using a plaster mould to produce several pieces at once allows more time for creative decoration*

JEANETTE ORRELL

·INTERIORS·

EMMA BOON

Candlestick, mirror, pen/pencil holder, bottle coaster and napkin ring

EQUIPMENT AND MATERIALS

Corrugated and plain cardboard	**Wrapping paper of fish or photocopies**
Masking tape	**Watercolour paints (optional)**
Newspapers, etc	
PVA/white glue	**Crackle varnish set**
White emulsion paint	**Matt varnish**
Brushes	**Fire retardant liquid**
Gouache and gold paints	**Small metal candle-holder**
	Mirror

METHOD For the candlestick roll a length of cardboard, corrugated side out, into a tube and secure with masking tape. From smooth cardboard cut out a large star and with PVA/white glue affix it to one end of the tube as a base. Cut a smaller star for the top rim, cut a hole in it so that it will slip over the top of the tube and glue it in place.

Using PVA/white glue, paste on five layers of newspaper pieces both inside (as far as possible) and outside.

When dry, coat the candlestick with white emulsion, followed by a layer of pale green paint. The top and bottom edges are painted gold.

Using watercolours, colour in the fish on the wrapping paper or photocopies (the latter may need to be given

a spray of fixative first). Cut out and glue on the fish. Next draw on and paint in some gold stars edged in waterproof ink.

To create a distressed appearance suggesting antiquity apply two layers of crackle varnish as per the maker's instructions. Once dry, apply a coat of matt varnish, plus a final coat of fire retardant inside and out. Lastly, insert the metal candle-holder in the top.

The pen/pencil holder, bottle coaster and napkin ring are made of smooth cardboard, using the same methods of construction and decoration as for the candlestick.

To make the mirror frame cut out a rectangle of thick, smooth cardboard, in the centre of which a rectangle is cut out slightly smaller than the piece of mirror. Around this central opening glue on flattened pasted rolls of newspaper to create a raised rim. Using PVA/white glue and masking tape, secure the mirror, face out, to the back of the cardboard.

Next cut a second rectangle of cardboard precisely the same size as the first and glue this on as a backing board to the mirror and cardboard front. Secure the edges with masking tape, if necessary. Then cover all the cardboard with at least four layers of pasted paper pieces.

Once dry, proceed to prime with emulsion, decorate and seal in the same manner as the candlestick. If any paint strays on to the mirror, this can be delicately scraped off with a scalpel.

Spice rack and stationery holder

EQUIPMENT AND MATERIALS

Cardboard	Newspapers, etc
Pencil or felt-tip pen	Bowl of wallpaper paste
Ruler	Ball of coarse string
Craft knife and scissors	White emulsion paint
PVA/white glue	Brushes
Masking tape	Gouache paints
Gummed paper tape	Matt varnish

METHOD For the two-shelf spice rack mark out on a sheet of cardboard with the aid of a pencil/pen and ruler the backing sheet, two matching end pieces, two matching shelf pieces and two identical front panels. With a craft knife cut out the backing piece and one each of the ends, the shelves and the fronts. Place the end, the shelf and the front piece on the outlines of their matching pairs, and check that the outlines and dimensions are the same. Cut out the second end, shelf and front pieces.

With PVA/white glue and masking tape secure the pieces together and leave to dry. Replace the masking tape with gummed paper tape for strength. Cover the whole rack with three layers of pasted paper pieces and set aside to dry. Then affix appropriate lengths of string to all external edges and joins with PVA/white glue and masking tape. When the glue is dry, cover the string and the rest of the rack with a layer of pasted paper pieces, taking care not to flatten the string too much while emphasizing its outline.

From cardboard cut out five hearts and cover them with a layer of pasted paper pieces, keeping the outline as crisp as possible. When they are dry, glue four to the front of the bottom shelf and one centre top.

Glue two curlicues of string to the upper part of the back panel and a further piece zig-zagging along the front of the top shelf. Cover all the string in a layer of pasted paper pieces and leave to dry.

Coat the rack with white emulsion before painting with watered gouaches and finally sealing with a matt varnish.

The stationery holder is made using the same techniques.

AMANDA BLUNDEN

Tulips in a blue jug

EQUIPMENT AND MATERIALS

For tulips:

2 packets long, medium-
  gauge stub/florists' wire

Wire-cutters/tin-snips

Newspapers

Bowl of flour and water
  paste or PVA/white glue

1 packet thick stub/florists'
  wire or poker wire

Fine sandpaper/glasspaper

White emulsion paint

Brushes

Poster paints or similar

Matt varnish

For jug:

Jug as a mould

Newspapers

Bowl of wallpaper paste

Scalpel

PVA/white glue

Masking tape

Gummed paper tape

Wire from old coathanger

White emulsion paint

Brushes

Gold and blue paint

Sponge

Semi-gloss varnish

METHOD Each individual tulip petal is made separately by bending a length of stub/florists' wire to shape and twisting the two ends together at the base of the petal – do not trim the ends. With PVA/white glue or paste stick long thin strips of newspaper round and across the wire frame, keeping the edges smooth and adjusting the shape as you proceed. Cover each petal with three layers of paper and set aside to dry.

In one hand hold the wire ends of five petals round a length of thick wire, and with your other hand wind a pasted or glued strip of newspaper round all the wires. Begin just below the base of the petals and spiral the paper gradually down the stem. Add further layers, but set aside to dry before the newspaper becomes too mushy. Add further layers until the wire stem is covered. Leave to dry and then, if necessary, smooth the surfaces with fine sandpaper/glasspaper.

Cover the whole flower and stalk with a coat of white emulsion. When that is dry, paint the petals and stalks in the shades of your choice and finally seal them with a coat of matt varnish.

Although jugs are usually based on layers of pasted newspaper pieces moulded on a balloon (see page 17), Melanie Williams often prefers to mould layers on an existing jug of attractive proportions. The outside of the jug and handle ends are covered in a layer of damp, unpasted newspaper pieces. Remember to leave paper protruding above the rim. Five or more layers of pasted paper pieces are then applied and left to dry.

Using a scalpel, delicately cut the paper jug vertically in half and remove it from the mould. Immediately stick the two halves together again with PVA/white glue, and secure in place with masking tape. When the join has dried, replace the masking tape with pieces of gummed paper tape for strength. Cover the joins with a layer of pasted paper pieces.

To smooth the rim, moisten the paper round it with paste and bend it over neatly. If necessary, apply one or more layers of pasted paper strips over the rim from inside to outside (see page 18).

Handles can be made in several ways (see page 23), but Melanie sometimes chooses to change the position and shape of the original handle, so she has her own method. She dampens the rough paper round the existing handle holes with wallpaper paste and folds it together to cover the gaps. If necessary, she adds fresh pasted paper pieces inside and out to create a smooth surface. The basis of the new handle is coathanger wire pushed into the jug through two small holes made with a scalpel. The wire ends are bent flat against the inside of the jug, secured with masking tape and pasted over with pieces of paper. The wire handle is then bound in layer upon layer of long pasted strips of paper and left to dry.

Following a coat of white emulsion paint, a layer of gold paint is applied. When that is dry, rich blue paint is sponged on. For protection the whole jug is given one or more coats of semi-gloss varnish.

These tulips in a jug were inspired by a Cézanne painting – why not try Van Gogh's sunflowers, for instance

Firescreen

Sheet of rigid board, e.g. medium-density fibre-board (MDF)

Pencil or felt-tip pen

Newspapers

Bowl of wallpaper paste

White emulsion paint

Brushes

Gouache paints

Wrapping paper or wallpaper

Oil glaze

Semi-gloss varnish

Jigsaw

Fine sandpaper/glasspaper

Metal hinges and pins

Hammer

METHOD On a sheet of rigid board sketch with a pencil or felt pen the outline of a firescreen to suit the dimensions of your fireplace.

Cover the area of the screen with a layer of pasted pieces of newspaper. Over the lower part which is going to look like a marble urn or vase apply a coat of white emulsion. When that is dry, paint on a stone-coloured background in gouache and add *trompe l'oeil* marble streaks. (Alternatively you could paste shop-bought marbled paper over this area instead.)

From floral wrapping paper or wallpaper tear out (do not cut) individual flowers, fruit, leaves or whatever.

Paste a selection of these, overlapping one slightly with another, over the rest of the screen. Work from the edge inwards and allow some pieces to overlap the 'marble' container.

When dry, in order to make the decoration appear more three-dimensional and as though it were hand-painted, paint shadows in blue-grey gouache on the fake vase, beneath the flowers, fruit, etc, which appear to overlap the 'container' and round the lower edges of the central pieces (see detail below).

Once the paint is dry, apply a coat of oil glaze. This is absorbed by the torn paper edges in particular and helps to heighten the antique, three-dimensional quality of the decoration. When this is dry, apply one or more coats of semi-gloss varnish, allowing each to dry before applying the next.

With a jigsaw cut round the outline of the screen and smooth any rough edges with fine sandpaper/glasspaper. Also cut out a triangle of board to attach to the back with a couple of metal hinges; this supports the screen.

After applying a coat of white emulsion to the edge and back of the screen, use gouache paints to decorate them in sympathetic colours. Seal them with a coat of varnish.

Lamp

EQUIPMENT AND MATERIALS

Several lengths of wood approx. 4cm (1½ in) square	Wire-cutters/tin-snips
	Pair of pliers
	Pair of protective gloves
Hammer and nails	Materials and equipment
Handsaw	for making pulp (see
Electrical wire	page 25)
Plastic or rubber tubing	PVA/white glue
Masking tape	Fine sandpaper/glasspaper
Metal lamp fittings and glass globes	White emulsion paint
	Brushes
Screwdriver and screws (for lamps)	Acrylic paints, oil pastels, etc
Chickenwire	Matt varnish

METHOD This lamp is about 1m (3½ ft) high and even Louise Vergette admits that it is a lengthy and fairly complex project.

Since large quantities of paper pulp cannot safely be supported by chickenwire alone, you have to begin by constructing a rough framework from wood. You need, for instance, one long piece for the neck and spine of the figure, a cross piece for the shoulders, two pieces of wood almost at right angles to each other for an arm; a cross piece for the hips, and a long piece for each leg which goes down to join a solid, irregularly shaped construction for the base. From the base one piece of wood also projects upwards from one side to support the jug-lamp.

Once the wooden framework is reasonably stable, thread two lengths of electrical wire through plastic or rubber tubing for protection. Wire up the two metal light fittings and screw one on to the end of the wooden frame where the raised hand will be and one to where the top of the jug will be.

With masking tape secure both lengths of wiring down the frame into the base so that they can emerge from the back.

From various lengths of chickenwire form the head with its hair, the body, arms and legs, a pair of wings on her back, plus the base, the jug and the protruding log. Shaping the chickenwire is a tricky process requiring time and patience. Turn any protruding spikes of wire inwards with the pliers.

When the shape seems reasonably satisfactory, make sufficient coarse paper pulp with PVA/white glue (not wallpaper paste) to cover the whole chickenwire frame in one layer. The pulp should be dryish and sticky. Louise Vergette applies the pulp straight on to the wire,

but you can, if you prefer, paste on a layer of paper pieces first. Apply the pulp in small handfuls, a bit at a time, then smooth the surface roughly and leave to dry.

Coat the pulp with diluted PVA/white glue to strengthen the structure. When that is dry, apply the next layer of pulp, shaping the contours of the sculpture and base as you proceed. Leave it to dry thoroughly before painting on another coat of diluted PVA/white glue.

Continue adding layers in this manner until the final coating, which must be of very fine pulp.

The drapery is then created from chickenwire covered in a layer of pasted newspaper pieces, which is in turn coated in very fine pulp. Smooth the surface of the sculpture with fine sandpaper/glasspaper.

The leaves on the log are cut from matt green plastic-coated material; they are glued to wire stalks, which are in turn glued into the final layer of damp pulp with PVA/white glue. If you forget to do this at the right moment, simply add a small quantity of fine pulp to the junction of the wire with the log.

The lizard is shaped freehand from fine pulp.

Cut a piece of cardboard to fill the bottom of the base and, before you secure it in place with PVA/white glue and masking tape, remember to make a hole in the back of the base and feed the wiring through it. Cover the base with a layer of fine pulp.

Allow at least four weeks for the whole structure to dry out before priming it with a coat of white emulsion paint. Louise Vergette then uses a mixture of paints, including acrylics and oil pastels, to colour her lamp. A coat of matt varnish adds protection.

Candlesticks, winged vase and bowl

EQUIPMENT AND MATERIALS

Sheets of rigid board or materials and equipment for making plaster moulds (see page 27)	Palette knife
	PVA/white glue
	Masking tape
	Rigid card or cardboard
Hammer, nails and plastic parcel tape (optional)	White emulsion paint
	Brushes
Soft soap or washing-up liquid	Acrylic, gouache or powder paints including gold
Materials and equipment for making pulp (see page 25)	
	Modelling clay (optional)
	Semi-gloss varnish
Fine sawdust (optional filling for pulp)	Fire retardant spray
	Metal candle-holder
Disposable cellulose cleaning cloths	

METHOD There are several ways in which these candlesticks may be formed, but Sue Sanders chooses to make them from flat sheets of dried pulp.

For the candlesticks, begin by making three shallow triangular moulds which are flat at the top and base – one for each side. The moulds can be made of plaster/gypsum in a large plastic tray, as shown on page 27, or formed from any kind of rigid sheets of board nailed and/or taped together with parcel tape. Cover the insides of the moulds with soft soap or washing-up liquid.

Next make a quantity of pulp from shredded newspapers, following the directions given on page 25, but adding more than usual PVA/white glue for strength and, if you wish, fine sawdust as a filler.

Remove any surplus water from the pulp so that it is dryish, but not too sticky. Pour it into the moulds to a depth of just under 0.5cm (¼in). With a disposable cellulose cleaning cloth rolled into a smooth pad, press the pulp firmly into place, compacting it and drying

it. Smooth the surface with a palette knife and set aside until it is dry.

Roll some more pulp into long thin sausages between the palms of your hands, bend them into coils and leave to dry flat.

Remove the dried sheets of pulp carefully and stick them together with PVA/white glue, temporarily secured by masking tape, which is removed once the glue is dry.

From rigid card or cardboard cut two triangles – one to fit the base and one, with a hole in the centre to accommodate a metal holder for the candle base, to fit the top. Glue them in place and, when dry, cover both with a thin coating of pulp. Check that the metal candle-holders still fit the holes. Leave to dry. Glue the three coils round the top rim and add some pulp to the top and bottom rims, pinching it to form a frilly edge.

After a coat of white emulsion, the candlesticks are given four or five thin coats of paint in varying shades of blue, darker in some areas than others. Allow each coat to dry before applying the next.

The shells, stars and nodules with which Sue adorns her pieces are made of plaster/gypsum cast in a series of plaster moulds lined with petroleum jelly, but you can, if you prefer, sculpt them from modelling clay. Either way, when dry, they are primed with emulsion, glued on and painted gold, as are the frilled rims. A coat of semi-gloss varnish is followed by a coat of fire retardant. Put the metal candle-holders in place.

The body of the vase is made from pulp, in two halves in two plaster moulds (see page 27). When dry, it is glued together with PVA/white glue, and a thin layer of pulp is smeared over the dry join to disguise it. The 'wings' are then shaped on the vase freehand from dryish pulp before sealing, decorating and varnishing in the same way as the candlesticks.

The small bowl is made of pulp moulded on the inside of an existing bowl and is completed by following the same steps as for the other objects.

Mantelpiece clocks

EQUIPMENT AND MATERIALS

Battery-operated clock
  mechanisms

Smooth cardboard with
  corrugated interior

Flexible card or cardboard

Pencil and metal ruler

Craft knife

PVA/white glue

Masking tape

Materials and equipment
  for making pulp (see
  page 25)

Newspapers

Bowl of wallpaper paste

Fine sandpaper/glasspaper

White emulsion paint

Brushes

Scalpel

Gouache paints

Semi-gloss varnish

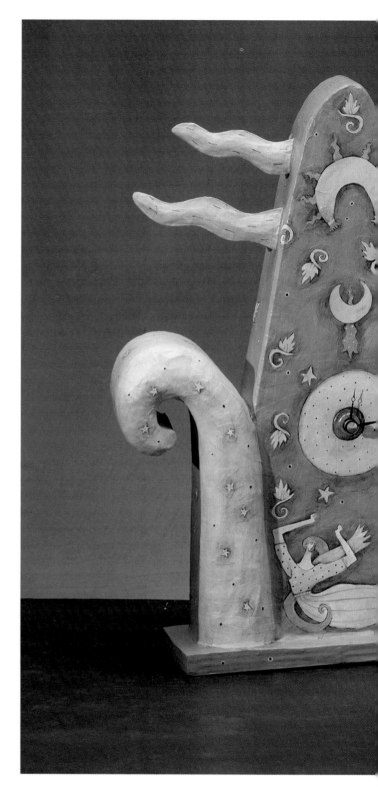

METHOD Both Juliette Pearce's unusual timepieces are made using the same basic techniques.

With a craft knife cut out two matching rectangles of cardboard and attach one on top of the other with PVA/white glue and masking tape – this forms the base.

For the case of the red clock cut out two matching triangles and two rectangles of cardboard. Check that the rectangles are sufficiently deep from front to back of the case to house the clock mechanism. In the triangle for the back cut a square hole slightly larger than the mechanism so that the battery can be easily changed when necessary. Attach the four pieces of the case to each other with PVA/white glue and masking tape, replacing the latter with gummed paper tape when the glue is dry. Attach the case to the base in the same way.

For the case of the blue clock cut two long triangles of matching size from cardboard and round off the top points. From flexible card or thin cardboard cut one strip sufficiently long to run round the two longest sides of the triangles – again check that the depth front to back is adequate to house the mechanism. Then proceed as for the red clock above.

The basis of the various shooting stars and horns on the clocks is cardboard cut to shape and secured to the case and base with PVA/white glue and masking tape. To prevent the cardboard from warping, paint it with diluted glue and leave to dry. Then apply several layers of dryish paper pulp. Allow the pulp to dry out and then lightly dampen its surface before applying the next layer. Continue until the forms are as you wish. Cover the final damp layer of pulp with a layer of pasted paper pieces and, as you do so, smooth the pulp beneath.

Also cover the cardboard case and base with two layers of pasted paper pieces. When all is dry, smooth any rough patches with sandpaper/glasspaper and apply a coat of emulsion.

When that is dry, with a scalpel make a neat hole in the face large enough to accommodate the hands' spindle and then draw and paint on the clock face and

JULIETTE PEARCE

other decorations. Seal the clock cases with semi-gloss varnish. Hold the clock mechanism behind the clock face, push the spindle through to the front and attach the hands; this will hold the lightweight mechanism securely in place.

Sunray mirror

EQUIPMENT AND MATERIALS

Mounting card or card-
    board

Flexible card

Scissors and craft knife

Pencil or felt pen

Masking tape

Materials and equipment
    for making pulp (see
    page 25)

Mixing bowls

Plaster of Paris/gypsum

Water

Palette knife (optional)

Brushes

Gouache paints

Metallic powder paint

Semi-gloss varnish

Mirror

PVA/white glue

METHOD Make an appropriate quantity of paper pulp for the size of mirror you require.

Cut a circle from a sheet of cardboard/card and cut a hole in the centre to hold the mirror. Using 1cm (½in) strips of flexible card, encircle both the outer and inner rims and fix these upright 'walls' firmly in place with masking tape.

Pour the pulp on to the cardboard base until it reaches the top of the encircling rims. Press the pulp down firmly, fill in any uneven patches and smooth the surface with a palette knife. Leave to dry for a week or so in a warm place.

Make a thick, creamy mix of plaster/gypsum with water in a mixing bowl, pour this in rays round the inner rim and then shape it more precisely with a palette knife or your fingers.

Once the plaster/gypsum is dry, Julie Howells creates an intricate patchwork pattern in gouache paints in three or more layers, often using a dotted pointillist technique on the final layer. The sun's rays are covered in several layers of metallic powder paint and the whole sealed with varnish. The mirror is cut to size and secured in place with PVA/white glue to the back of the frame.

The two bowls are made from pulp shaped on conical moulds and each is supported by three balls of pulp.

JULIE HOWELLS

Gargoyle

EQUIPMENT AND MATERIALS

Shredded scrap paper, newspapers, etc	Plaster of Paris/gypsum
Vat or dustbin of hot water	Wooden stirring implement
Mixer-blender	Spoon
PVA/white glue	Wooden spatula
Materials and equipment for making paper (see page 34) or shop-bought handmade paper	Sponge
	Sheet of chipboard or medium-density fibreboard (MDF)
2 sheets of plywood	Jigsaw or hacksaw
Modelling clay	Brushes
Kitchen knives, sculpting tools, etc	White emulsion paint
Soft soap or washing-up liquid	Brass-rubbing sticks, acrylic paints, wax crayons, wax-based gold paint, etc
4 planks of wood	Spray can of semi-gloss varnish
Strong adhesive tape or parcel tape	
Large container of water	

METHOD Since Emma Halsall's gargoyle, as she calls it, is about 91.5cm (3ft) in length and many of her other creations are fairly large, she obtains shredded scrap paper in bulk from the local council. After checking that no plastic is mixed in with it, the paper is put into a large container of hot water and left to soak for several hours. Then it is blended into pulp in a commercial mixer-blender and only a substantial quantity of PVA/white glue is added – nothing else. (Quantities are inevitably a matter of trial and error or, as in Emma's case, experience.) Make some of the pulp into sheets of paper (see page 34).

Meanwhile, on a large board, shape modelling clay by hand into a rough gargoyle shape and leave it to set for about a day until it is leathery hard. Then sculpt in details with kitchen knives or other implements. Coat the carved clay with soft soap or washing-up liquid (*not* petroleum jelly), especially in any nooks and crannies.

Using planks of wood secured at the corners with strong tape, build a 'retaining wall' round the clay sculpture; fill any gaps in the 'wall' with clay. Check that the top of the 'wall' is at least 2.5cm (1in) higher than the top of the clay sculpture. (If the plaster mould you are about to make is too thin, it will break.) Cover the insides of the 'wall' with soft soap or washing-up liquid.

Fill a large container with water and pour in plaster of Paris/gypsum powder until a peak appears above the surface. Leave it for one minute so that any air bubbles are evacuated and then stir the mixture gently with a wooden implement – do not whisk. The mixture will begin to give off warmth as it 'goes off', i.e. is ready to use. Spoon some of the mixture over the details in the sculpture before steadily pouring on the rest until it almost reaches the top of the 'retaining wall'.

When the plaster/gypsum feels cold, it should be set, but leave it a while longer to be on the safe side. Cover the area of plaster/gypsum with another large board and carefully turn the whole 'sandwich' of board, plaster/gypsum, clay and base board upside down.

Ease the planks away from the edge of the mould and gently remove the clay, using a wooden spatula or similar to extract the fiddly bits. Take care not to damage the new mould.

Line the inside of the mould with a slightly dampened sheet of handmade paper, easing it into the crannies with a sponge. In the same way add a second layer of paper. Then squeeze a handful of pulp to remove the water and press it into the mould with your fingertips. Once several handfuls have been applied, press the pulp down with a sponge to compact it and remove excess moisture. Continue to fill the mould in this manner until the pulp spreads over the edge of the mould. Put it somewhere warm and airy until the pulp is only slightly damp and adheres together – it must not be totally dry or it will stick to the mould.

Turn the mould upside down on a clean board and very gently ease the pulp sculpture out all the way round – use a wooden spatula, if necessary. Leave until the pulp is completely dry.

To strengthen the gargoyle, outline its shape with a pencil on to a sheet of chipboard or MDF and cut this out with a saw. Coat both the flat back of the gargoyle and one face of the board with PVA/white glue and stick them together. When the glue is dry, cover the join and board edges neatly with a layer of paper pulp, and leave to dry.

Coat the entire gargoyle with white emulsion. Once that is dry, decorate it as you will – brass-rubbing sticks are particularly effective, as are sponged on watercolours. Finally spray on a coat of semi-gloss varnish.

Cupboard and shelves

EQUIPMENT AND MATERIALS

Planks of wood approx 1cm (½in) thick.	Newspapers, etc
Backing board approx 0.5cm (¼in) thick or sheets of corrugated cardboard	Bowl of wallpaper paste
	Rigid poker wire and wire-cutters/tin-snips
Tape measure and pencil	White emulsion paint
Handsaw	Brushes
Craft knife	Gouache paints
Hammer and nails	Waterproof black ink
PVA/white glue	Metal hinges and pins (for cupboard)
Masking tape	Gloss polyurethane varnish
Gummed paper tape	

METHOD Jeanette Orrell prefers to recycle materials whenever possible, so the frames of her cupboard and shelves are made from driftwood. However, they can equally well be made of two layers of cardboard stuck together with PVA/white glue and masking tape; once the glue is dry, the masking tape should be replaced by gummed paper tape.

For the shelves, cut a backing board from wood or cardboard approximately 84cm (33in) high × 30.5cm (12in) wide and with a saw or craft knife round one end to a semi-circle, leaving 61cm (24in) of straight sides below.

Cut two rectangles for the sides, each 61cm × 12.5cm (24in × 5in), and four shelves each 30.5cm × 12.5cm (12in × 5in). If you are using wood, nail the pieces together. If the frame is of cardboard, secure the pieces with PVA/white glue and masking tape, replacing the latter with gummed paper tape once the glue is dry. Then paint the unit with diluted white glue to prevent the cardboard warping. Cover the whole construction with three layers of pasted paper pieces and leave to dry.

Cut a bird or other appealing shape from cardboard and affix a short length of rigid wire both to the bottom of the bird and to the back of the shelves using PVA/white glue and masking tape. When the glue is dry, cover the bird with three layers of pasted paper pieces and the top of the back of the shelves with two layers. Leave to dry.

Coat the shelves and the bird with two layers of emulsion paint. When they are dry, draw your design in pencil, paint on the background and foreground colours, and then outline the design in ink. Seal with one or more coats of gloss polyurethane varnish.

With the proviso that wood makes a stronger frame on which to hang a door, the cupboard is made using the same techniques as the shelves. The back panel is, of course, shaped differently at the top and, to fit this shape, the side panels are curved into a quarter circle at the top.

Complete the shelves and door up to the stage where they are ready to varnish. Secure the two hinges to the inside of the door and to the front surface of the shelf upright with both PVA/white glue and nails or pins. Finally give the inside and outside of the cupboard one or more coats of varnish.

If you are not good at drawing, use black-and-white photocopies coloured with crayons or paint

Clock and mirrors

EQUIPMENT AND MATERIALS

For clock:

Chickenwire
Wire-cutters/tin-snips
Pair of pliers
Newspapers
Bowl of wallpaper paste
Pencil and metal ruler
A4-size black-and-white
  photocopies
Poster paints, gouache, etc

Brushes
Semi-gloss varnish
Battery-powered or
  quartz clock mechanism
For mirrors:
As above plus
Mirror
Plastic sheeting
Masking tape
PVA/white glue

METHOD Roll out a length of chickenwire and cut out a square the same as the width of the roll. With pliers tuck in the spiky wire ends and then bend the chickenwire into folds. For the tassel bend a small, loose roll of chickenwire to shape and attach it by its raw edge.

Cover both sides of the wire with one layer of pasted pieces of newspaper.

On one or more sheets of plain A4 paper draw your own design to photocopy, or photocopy images from books. Colour the photocopies and, when dry, tear each into four pieces. Paste the pieces in a random patchwork over the front and back of the frame.

On a small square of plain paper draw out and paint a clock face; glue this to the centre of the frame. Make a small hole in the centre of the face to accommodate the clock hands and, before attaching the clock mechanism, paint the whole frame with a coat of semi-gloss varnish.

The mirrors are made in similar fashion by folding in the edges of a chickenwire square or rectangle by about 1cm (½in) as a 'hem' and then, having made 4cm (1½in) cuts bisecting the corners, fold the edges another 4cm (1½in) all round. For the lower mirror in the picture attach a hemmed triangle of chickenwire by one raw edge and add a roll shaped like a tassel. Then cut a hole of appropriate shape in the centre to house the mirror; fold in the spiky edges. Cover the frame with one layer of pasted newspaper pieces and a layer of painted photocopies (see above). With PVA/white glue secure the mirror to the back of the frame. Then cover the back with a sheet of plastic (to protect the mirror) affixed with masking tape, and cover this with two layers of pasted newspaper pieces plus a layer of coloured photocopies. When dry, seal the whole with semi-gloss varnish.

Trinket cupboard, hand mirror and box

EQUIPMENT AND MATERIALS

Materials and equipment for making a plaster mould (see page 27)	Brushes
Soft soap or washing-up liquid	Acrylic, gouache or powder paints
Materials and equipment for making pulp (see page 25)	Semi-gloss varnish
	Modelling clay (optional)
Fine sawdust (optional filler for pulp)	Kitchen knives, sculpting implements, etc
	Gold paint
Mirror	Hacksaw or jigsaw
PVA/white glue	Masking tape
	Metal hinges, door catch and pins (for cupboard)
White emulsion paint	Small hammer

METHOD The basic components of all three objects shown opposite are sheets of paper pulp just under 0.5cm (¼in) thick.

The hand mirror is the simplest to start with. First of all make a shallow plaster/gypsum mould, following the directions given on page 27. It must be triangular in shape with rounded corners and sealed with a coating of soft soap or washing-up liquid.

Make a quantity of paper pulp, following the recipe on page 25, but containing more PVA/white glue than wallpaper paste and, if you wish, fine sawdust instead of ground chalk/whiting as the filler. The aim is for the resulting sheet of pulp to be dense and rigid.

Pour off any surplus water from the pulp (ideally there should be none) and tip it into the prepared mould until the pulp is about 0.5cm (¼in) deep.

To the centre of the triangular sheet of dried pulp affix a square mirror with PVA/white glue. When that is dry, build up fingerfuls of dryish pulp round the edge of the mirror and the edge of the frame, pinching it into shape.

Once the edges are dry, apply a coat of white emulsion and then five thin coats of paint, graduated to darker shades round the edges.

Sue Sanders casts her ornamental shells, starfish and nodules in plaster in a series of plaster moulds protected with a coating of soft soap or washing-up liquid, but you can, if you prefer, sculpt them in modelling clay. When dry, they are coated in emulsion and then glued to the frame. A coat of gold paint is then applied. If any paint, etc, strays on to the mirror, it can be removed delicately with the tip of a scalpel.

The box is made from six sheets of pulp. When the four sheets which form the sides are dry, cut an irregular line horizontally through them with a jigsaw. Make sure these halves are correctly matched when you glue the pieces together. Until the glue is dry, secure the joins with masking tape, then remove it. Prime, decorate and finally varnish the box as you did the mirror.

The components of the trinket cupboard are also sheets of pulp. If the pulp is dense enough, all the flat parts – the back, sides, roof, doors, shelves and angled feet – can be cut with a fine hacksaw or jigsaw from a single large sheet. Otherwise each piece will have to be shaped individually in a plaster mould (see above). In either case, the curved brackets are best shaped from pulp in a plaster mould, although it is possible to shape them freehand. The components are stuck together with PVA/white glue, secured temporarily by masking tape until the glue is dry. After removing the tape, the cupboard is primed with emulsion, painted, varnished and ornamented in the same manner as the mirror. Finally the hinges and door catch are pinned in place.

Wall sconce

EQUIPMENT AND MATERIALS

Smooth, thick cardboard	White emulsion paint
Pencil	Brushes
Craft knife	Acrylic paints
Gummed paper tape	Gloss varnish
PVA/white glue	Fire retardant spray or
Mirror and glass-cutter	liquid
Masking tape	Metal candle-holder with
String	spike

METHOD Draw the outline of the sconce, including the hole behind the bird's head, on a sheet of cardboard and cut it out with a craft knife. Lay this on a second sheet of cardboard, trace the outline in pencil and cut it out. In the first sheet of cardboard cut a circle near the top and bind the edge neatly with strips of gummed paper tape to create a smooth rim.

To the back of the first sheet of cardboard glue a circle of mirror facing the front through the hole near the top. Then attach the top layer of cardboard firmly to the second layer with PVA/white glue and strips of masking tape. Cut the rest of the mirror into various shapes and glue the pieces to the front surface. Glue string round them to create a raised rim, and glue on string anywhere else you wish to form ridges.

To support the candle-holder cut five pieces of cardboard to form a pyramidal box – the back is part of the existing sconce. Keep trimming them with a craft knife until the pieces fit neatly. Then secure the joins with PVA/white glue and masking tape.

Cover the string and all the cardboard front and back with strips of gummed paper tape, moulding it neatly round edges and ridges.

Paint the sconce with white emulsion. If any marks the pieces of mirror, carefully scrape it off with the point of a scalpel.

Decorate the sconce in acrylic paints. When they are dry, coat the sconce with gloss varnish and fire retardant. Lastly fix the tiny spiked candle-holder in place with PVA/white glue.

KATIE WALLIS

Dressing-table mirror

EQUIPMENT AND MATERIALS

Corrugated cardboard	White emulsion paint
Craft knife	Brushes
PVA/white glue	Gouache and gold paints
Masking tape	Fine sandpaper/glasspaper
Gummed paper tape	Materials for making pulp
Newspapers, etc	(see page 25)
Bowl of wallpaper paste	Semi-gloss varnish
Piece of mirror	Real limpet shells

METHOD Cut three squares of cardboard of equal size. In two of them cut a square in the centre and glue these two layers together, one on top of the other. Secure with masking tape until dry; then replace with gummed paper tape. Coat all the pieces with diluted PVA/white glue to prevent warping. Cover the front of the frame and inner rim only with four layers of pasted paper pieces. Leave to dry.

Meanwhile, using PVA/white glue and masking tape, secure the mirror to the centre of the cardboard backing panel and leave to dry. Then secure the backing panel with the mirror to the back of the front frame.

Cover the sides and back of the mirror frame with three smooth layers of pasted paper pieces. Once dry, paint the whole frame with three coats of emulsion.

Paint the whole frame pale green and, when dry, rub some of the paint off with sandpaper/glasspaper to give an antique look. Paint a line of gold round the outer and inner rims.

The starfish and large seashells are moulded freehand from pulp (see page 27), dried in a tray of coarse sand, then painted and glued to the frame together with genuine shells. Lastly apply a coat of semi-gloss varnish to the frame and ornaments.

Throne

EQUIPMENT AND MATERIALS

Several large sheets of plywood

Pencil

Tape measure

Sheet of chipboard or medium-density fibre-board (MDF)

Handsaw

Hammer, nails and pins

PVA/white glue

Chickenwire

U-shaped pins

Newspapers

Cardboard

Bowl of wallpaper paste

Modelling plastic

Masking tape

Materials and equipment for making pulp (see page 25)

Acrylic gesso

Brushes

Spray cans of metallic paint

Emulsion and acrylic paints

Softwood, e.g. balsa

Flexible reel wire

METHOD On a large sheet of plywood mark out a pointed oval shape with a flat base approximately 45.5cm (18in) wide. Around the top half of the pointed oval, draw pointed spikes. Cut out the whole of the back including the spikes.

To form the seat cut four pieces of chipboard or MDF 45.5cm (18in) square and nail them into a box which is open on two sides, i.e. front and back.

The flat front of the seat and arms is cut from a single sheet of plywood, and two rectangular pieces of plywood comprise the flat-topped armrests on either side of the seat. The square seat frame of chipboard or MDF is nailed to the large plywood panel comprising the back of the throne.

Next the throne front and armrests are attached to the back of the throne with eighteen plywood struts secured with pins and PVA/white glue: three on each inside arm and six on each outside curve.

Four lengths of chickenwire are then stretched over the two inside curves of the armrests and two on the outside curves. Secure the chickenwire in place with U-pins.

The curved, dome-shaped back of the throne (not visible in the illustration) is formed by a chickenwire armature firmly padded out with masses of crumpled newspaper and cardboard, and all attached to the plywood with U-pins.

To give the front face of the throne's seat and arms a padded appearance chickenwire cut to the same shape as the front panel, but slightly larger, is partially attached to the plywood with U-pins, stuffed with crumpled newspapers and then completely U-pinned to the frame.

Cover the whole throne with at least four layers of pasted paper pieces, allowing each layer to dry before applying the next.

The raised arch beneath the points on the back of the throne is shaped on a flat work surface out of modelling plastic, which is then covered in petroleum jelly. Four layers of pasted paper pieces are moulded on to it. Once the paper is dry, remove the paper arch from the mould and attach it to the throne with PVA/white glue and masking tape.

The balls on each side of the throne are formed from newspaper crumpled and rolled into spheres, taped into shape and pushed on to nails in the sides of the frame.

The rams' horns are formed of a long triangle of chickenwire bent into a cone, twisted into a spiral and coated in four layers of pasted paper pieces. They are then attached to the armrests with U-pins.

Paint the whole throne with a coat of diluted PVA/white glue to strengthen and seal it. Leave it to dry.

In the meantime make a substantial quantity of paper pulp, using PVA/white glue instead of wallpaper paste, so that it is dryish and sticky.

Using modelling plastic and/or twisted rolls of newspaper, model relief patterns all over the throne, front and back. Other relief patterns can be modelled in the paper pulp with which you now coat the entire throne. Leave for two to three weeks to dry out completely.

Next the throne is painted with three coats of acrylic gesso or with a mixture of diluted PVA/white glue and plaster of Paris/gypsum or ground chalk/whiting, allowing each layer to dry before applying the next.

Mary Fellows's throne is decorated with spray cans of six metallic colours, followed by touches of household and acrylic paints, leaving some metallic colours to show through. The finishing touches are provided by fanciful shapes sculpted in balsa wood with a craft knife, covered in pulp, decorated in metallic or acrylic paints and attached on wobbling wires to the back of the throne with U-pins.

·FUN AND GAMES·

MARIE GREGORY

Marine chess set

EQUIPMENT AND MATERIALS

Newspapers	White emulsion paint
Bowl of special paper	Brushes
paste for papier mâché	Gouache paints
(from craft shop)	Semi-gloss varnish
Modelling clay	Cardboard
Modelling tools, kitchen	Pencil and metal ruler
knives, etc	Craft knife
PVA/white glue	

METHOD Instead of traditional black and white chess pieces, each 'side' in this amazing chess set is comprised of eight prawns (pawns), two sea anemones on rocks (castles), two seahorses (knights), two puffer fish (bishops), a mermaid queen and a merman king.

The prawns are simplest to tackle first since they are made of rolls of pasted newspaper curled into a spiral and laid flat to dry. To prevent them unrolling and to create a flat base, press their undersides gently against a smooth, solid object. As with the other pieces, detailed features – in this case eyes and whiskers – are delicately shaped from modelling clay attached with PVA/white glue.

The anemones' rock bases and the main bodies of all the other pieces are made of large pieces of pasted newspaper crumpled into an appropriate form. They are then finely shaped by numerous layers of small pasted paper pieces. They will take several days to dry.

From modelling clay sculpt all the detailed features, such as the kings' beards, faces, hair, crowns and arms; the queens' faces, hair, crowns, breasts and arms; the puffer fishes' eyes, lips and dorsal fins; the seahorses' noses, eyes and fins; the sea anemones; and the bases of the pieces, where necessary. Some details can be moulded directly on to the paper bodies, others may be made separately and then glued on. Experiment – there are no hard and fast rules.

All the pieces are primed with emulsion before being painted a distinguishing basic colour for each 'team' and then sealed with semi-gloss varnish.

The board is made of two square pieces of cardboard, one about 2.5cm (1in) smaller than the other, secured together with PVA/white glue and masking tape. Copy the dimensions of the chequered area from a traditional chess or draughts board. Two layers of pasted paper pieces cover the cardboard and are allowed to dry before emulsioning, painting and finally coating with one or more layers of varnish.

Puppet theatre

For theatre:

Smooth cardboard with
  corrugated interior

Pencil and metal ruler

Craft knife

PVA/white glue

Masking tape

Gummed paper tape

Newspapers

Bowl of wallpaper paste

White emulsion paint

Brushes

Gouache paints

Waterproof black ink

Gloss polyurethane
  varnish

Black insulating tape

Red velvet (for front
  curtains)

Gold string (for curtain
  ties)

Black felt (for back
  curtain)

For glove puppet:

Modelling plastic

Petroleum jelly

Newspapers

Bowl of wallpaper paste

Scalpel

PVA/white glue

Masking tape

Gummed paper tape

White emulsion paint

Brushes

Gouache paints

Gloss polyurethane
  varnish

Red material

Scissors

Needle and thread

Gold braid

METHOD The base of the theatre is a solid box approximately 61cm × 30.5cm × 61cm (24in × 12in × 24in), cut from cardboard using the techniques described on page 28. Cover the base with three layers of pasted pieces of newspaper before joining it to the superstructure.

The superstructure, also of cardboard, is approximately 56cm wide × 25.5cm deep × 76.5cm high (22in × 10in × 30in). The whole of the front of the proscenium arch, including the curtain pelmet and 'footlights', is cut out all in one piece. There are two side pieces approximately 61cm high × 25.5cm wide (24in × 10in), and a strip of 56cm × 7.5cm (22in × 3in) joining the tops of the two side pieces at the back. Join all these pieces using the same method as for the base, and cover inside and out with three layers of pasted paper pieces.

Secure the superstructure to the base in the same manner and cover the joins with two layers of pasted paper strips. Cover everything in a coat of white emulsion. When that is dry, outline the decorative patterns in pencil, paint them in, outline them in ink and finally coat the theatre in varnish.

Secure the curtains of gathered red velvet to the back of the arch with insulating tape or similar. The black back curtain is in one piece, but has a slit cut in the middle to allow puppets through; this, too, is secured with tape to the inside of the back cross piece.

The crowned head of the puppet king is shaped first in modelling plastic. When it looks convincing, cover the mould with petroleum jelly and apply five layers of small pasted paper pieces. When these are dry, cut round the rim of the crown with a scalpel and remove it. Then make a vertical cut just behind each ear and remove the two halves. Immediately glue the three pieces together with PVA/white glue and masking tape. Replace the latter with gummed paper tape when the glue is dry.

After a coat of emulsion, paint the head using gouache colours and waterproof ink for the lines. Two coats of gloss varnish seal and protect the head.

Fashion the glove from red fabric and attach it to the head by turning the glove inside out and sewing repeatedly round the fabric neck and through the head. Finally, trim it with gold braid.

Helmet, hat and crombie

EQUIPMENT AND MATERIALS

Balloon (for helmet)

Bowl as mould (for hat
  and crombie)

Newspapers, etc

Bowl of wallpaper paste

Pliable cardboard or card

Masking tape

Modelling plastic or clay

Pencil

Craft knife

White emulsion paint

Brushes

Gouache and gold paints

Tartan wrapping paper

Semi-gloss and gloss
  varnish

Tissue paper

METHOD For Marion Elliot's intergalactic helmet, follow the directions given on page 17 on how to mould pasted paper on a balloon. Put on at least eight layers and set aside to dry.

To make the spikes, roll strips of cardboard or card into cones and tape them to the helmet with masking tape. Strengthen the joins with tiny strips of modelling plastic or clay and cover the whole area with three layers of pasted paper pieces.

When the helmet in dry, cut two eye holes with a craft knife and neaten the rims by pasting on small strips of paper. Set aside to dry. Paint the helmet with white emulsion inside and out, and, when that is dry, decorate it in lively colours and false eyes. Seal the helmet with a coat of semi-gloss varnish.

To make Marie Gregory's hat and crombie choose a mixing bowl mould that will fit easily on your head, allowing for the fact that pasted paper shrinks as it dries. Following the directions on page 13 for layering paper on an existing mould, build up eight layers of pasted paper pieces. Flatten the crown of the crombie by gently pressing the damp paper on to a flat surface and set aside to dry.

Add a flat rim to either hat by following the directions on page 19. Soften the shape of the brims by manipulating the damp cardboard/card and layers of pasted paper.

Leave both creations to dry before covering the crombie with a layer of tartan wrapping paper and a coat of gloss varnish, while the hat is covered with several layers of pasted crumpled pink tissue paper tinted with watery gouache paints. The flower stem is created from rolled tissue paper and the flower head of cardboard or card covered in more tissue paper. Glue the flower to the hat and, if you wish, seal it with spray matt varnish.

Finally pray for fine weather.

MARION ELLIOT AND MARIE GREGORY

FUN AND GAMES

115

Satyr, sphinx and Minotaur icons

EQUIPMENT AND MATERIALS

Cardboard

Pencil and metal ruler

Scalpel

PVA/white glue

Brush

Masking tape

Gummed paper tape

Newspapers

Bowl of wallpaper paste

Materials and equipment
  for making pulp (see
  page 25) or modelling
  plastic

White emulsion paint

Paint brushes

Gouache paints

Waterproof black ink

Gloss varnish

METHOD The techniques used in making the sphinx are almost precisely the same as for the other two.

With pencil and ruler mark on cardboard the six pieces for the solid box base, cut them out with a scalpel and secure the joins with PVA/white glue and strips of masking tape. Replace the latter with gummed paper tape for strength once the glue is dry. Cover the base with two layers of pasted paper pieces.

Next mark out on cardboard the proscenium arch, pointed cornice and star as one piece, plus two side pieces, a back sheet, and a rectangle which will form a flat roof behind the cornice. Cut them out carefully and join in the manner described above.

Mould the raised edge and plaque on the cornice (or any other feature you wish to add) from pulp or modelling plastic and then cover all the surfaces with two layers of pasted paper pieces.

When these are dry, affix the superstructure to the centre of the base with PVA/white glue, masking tape and then gummed paper tape. When dry, cover the joins with a layer of pasted paper pieces. Leave to dry before painting everything with white emulsion, outlining the pattern in pencil, and decorating in gouache and ink.

Draw the sphinx's outline, including two tabs beneath her legs, on cardboard and cut it out. Cover her in a layer of small pasted paper pieces, model her bulging legs in pulp or plastic, and then apply another layer of pasted paper pieces. Once dry, paint with a coat of emulsion. When that is dry, draw her form and features in pencil, paint them in gouache and outline them in ink. With a scalpel, cut two slits for the tabs in the base, put PVA/white glue on the tabs and on the bottom edge of the sphinx, and slot her into place. A tiny roll of modelling plastic running along the join behind the sphinx helps to keep her in place.

Finally paint everything with one or more coats of varnish.

MARION ELLIOT

My family dog and other animals

EQUIPMENT AND MATERIALS

Fine-gauge chickenwire

Wire-cutters/tin-snips

Pair of pliers

Protective gloves

Newspapers, etc

Bowl of wallpaper paste

PVA/white glue

Coarse sewing needle

White emulsion paint

Brushes

Poster paints or similar

Coarse nylon string,
  various colours

Scissors

Fine sandpaper/glasspaper

Matt varnish

METHOD The lifesize dog opposite (a portrait of a beloved family pet now departed) plus the smaller horse, cow and sheep above are all created from a chickenwire armature covered with up to eight layers of pasted paper pieces, using the techniques described on page 30.

The horse's mane and tail are devised from remnants of an old fancy-dress nylon wig. However, as in the case of the cow's tail, they can equally well be made from unravelled nylon string attached with PVA/white glue.

As an alternative, the sheep, a simple, solid shape with or without its base, can be made from paper pulp in a plaster mould (see page 27).

Whether they are ornaments for the home, set around a Christmas crib in church or are part of a toy farm-yard, such animals have a naïve charm.

Christmas tree decorations

EQUIPMENT AND MATERIALS

Cardboard

Pencil or felt-tip pen

Craft knife and scalpel

Red plastic-coated wire

Masking tape

Newspapers, etc

Bowl of wallpaper paste

White emulsion paint

Waterproof black felt-tip
  pen or ink

Brushes

Gouache paints

Ribbon

Materials and equipment
  for making pulp (see
  page 25)

Semi-gloss varnish

METHOD Traditional glass baubles (which could easily have been made from paper pulp coated with pearlized and metallic paints) provide an effective foil for Jeanette Orrell's cardboard folk art decorations and Melanie Williams's mustachioed Edwardian.

Having drawn a variety of shapes on a sheet of cardboard, Jeanette cuts them out with a scalpel or craft knife. A small loop of red wire is attached to the top of each with masking tape before the cardboard is covered with several layers of pasted paper pieces. When the paper is dry, a coat of white emulsion is applied to both sides. Once that is dry, the outline and any patterns are marked on in black ink and filled in with translucent shades of gouache paint. A length of silk ribbon is threaded through each loop to hang the decoration on the tree.

The lone portrait of a man with a moustache – one of a series loosely depicting Melanie's friends – makes a novel conversation piece. Cut out a small circle of cardboard and, on top of it, mould paper pulp freehand into the desired shape. (To make a large number of such decorations you could easily create a trayful of plaster moulds – see page 27.) With the aid of a scalpel, the end of a short piece of red wire for a loop was inserted through a tiny hole in the cardboard and damp pulp. When the paper is dry, a coat of white emulsion is painted on. When that too is dry, use gouache paints to create the decoration of your choice and finally seal the bauble with semi-gloss varnish.

JEANETTE ORRELL AND MELANIE WILLIAMS

Dolls

EQUIPMENT AND MATERIALS

Newspapers, etc	Scissors
Bowl of wallpaper paste	Kapok stuffing
PVA/white glue	Needle and thread
Materials and equipment for making pulp (see page 25)	Paints
	Brushes
	Semi-gloss varnish
Dressmaking pin	Material and button (for skirt)
Calico (for body)	

METHOD The arms and legs can be formed from pulp, but Melanie Williams prefers to make them by rolling pasted newspaper strips of appropriate width into tight tubes. Round off the ends of them with tiny pieces of pasted paper and set aside to dry.

To create a smooth doll's head, roll a good dollop of dryish, sticky pulp between the palms of your hands to form a perfect sphere and leave it to dry for several days.

For the neck, roll a narrow strip of pasted newspaper into a tight tube. When it is dry, embed the blunt head of a dressmaking pin into one end with a tiny blob of PVA/white glue and the pointed end with glue into the pulp head.

Melanie likes her dolls to have flexible bodies, so she makes them of fabric cut in an hour-glass shape, stuffed with kapok and painted with mocks frills, etc. However, the body can be shaped freehand from pulp, if you prefer.

Coat the head, neck, arms and legs in white emulsion before painting the features and accessories. Two coats of semi-gloss varnish are recommended to protect the head and limbs.

As you sew up the top and bottom of the stuffed body with a coarse needle and strong thread, attach the limbs and neck by stitching through them too. For the wrap-round skirt a small rectangle of material is gathered on one long side and a waistband is sewn over it. A tiny decorative button is attached to the centre front. Hem the skirt and then, on the under side of the waistband, stitch the skirt to the body.

MELANIE WILLIAMS

Dinosaurs

EQUIPMENT AND MATERIALS

Lengths of wood approx
  61cm × 5cm (24in × 2in)

Handsaw

Hammer and nails

Newspapers

Masking tape

Bowl of wallpaper paste

Latex (liquid rubber)

Brushes

Acrylic paints

PVA/white glue

METHOD All three dinosaurs – the long-necked Diplodocus, the spiky green Triceratops, and the Tyrannosaurus Rex – are all made in the same way, though their forms, of course, vary.

When his young son developed an interest in dinosaurs, Jean-Marc Faure made a couple of small ones to amuse him. Then he found he enjoyed making them, and – like Topsy and indeed, the little boy – they 'just growed'.

A simple, rough but sturdy skeleton of wood is constructed, on to which crumpled newspaper is tightly bound with masking tape. Further layers are added until a satisfactory form is achieved. Then apply a smooth layer of pasted paper pieces.

Once that is dry, paint the whole dinosaur with one or more coats of latex, allowing each to dry before applying the next.

Paint the dinosaur in appropriate acrylic colours and, when dry, apply one or more protective coats of diluted PVA/white glue.

JEAN-MARC FAURE

Toys

EQUIPMENT AND MATERIALS

Battered or secondhand self-winding mechanical cars, etc	Newspapers
	Bowl of wallpaper paste
	Black and red plastic-coated paper
Chickenwire	
Wire-cutters/tin-snips	Acrylic paints
Pair of pliers	Scalpel
Fine reel wire	PVA/white glue

METHOD When children grow tired of an old toy, this is an ingenious way of giving it a new lease of life. Even adults find these mechanized insects amusing.

Cut a rough circle of chickenwire and bend it into a dome. Curve the edge round the under side of the original mechanized toy and fix the chickenwire in place underneath with fine reel wire, taking care not to impede the self-winding mechanism and any wheels, etc. Use pliers to tuck any spiky wire ends safely away.

Cover the chickenwire armature with at least five layers of pasted paper pieces. When dry, attach legs and feelers cut from black plastic-coated paper to the sides and front with PVA/white glue. Then add another layer of small pasted paper pieces.

For smooth insects, decorate the body in several layers of bright acrylic paint, followed by a coat of gloss varnish.

If, on the other hand, you wish to create a furry-looking red and black bug, cut broad strips of black and red plastic-coated paper and into these make numerous vertical cuts to form a fringe. Using PVA/white glue, affix these 'fringes' in alternate overlapping bands round the body.

MIDGE LUCAS

LIST OF MAKERS

The following artists living in the UK kindly loaned their work to be photographed in this book:

Amanda Blunden; Emma Boon; Gerry Copp, School Cottage, Aisthorpe, Lincoln LN1 2SG; Marion Eliot; Jean-Marc Faure, 4 St Luke's Road, London W11 1DP; Mary Fellows; Caroline Gibbs; Amanda Godden; Marie Gregory, 180 Broomwood Road, London SW11 6JY; Emma Halsall; Maureen Hamilton-Hill, 56a King Henry's Road, London SW3 3RP; Carol Hill, Arcadia, Cotmandene, Dorking, Surrey; Cas Holmes, 123 York Road, Maidstone, Kent ME15 7QX; Julie Howells; Midge Lucas; Jenny Neame; Jeanette Orrell, 2 Cygnet Street, Poolstock, Wigan WN3 5BW; Paper Roses, 24 Milverton Terrace, Leamington Spa, Warwickshire CV32 5BA; Juliette Pearce; Louise Pearson, 1 Hall Cottages, Crazies Hill, Wargrave, Berkshire; Sue Sanders; Nicola Sargent; Malcolm Temple; Pam Tipping; Miriam Troth; Louise Vergette; Katie Wallis; and Melanie Williams. Antique pieces from Valerie Wade, 108 Fulham Road, London SW3 6HS.